The Poor of the Land

A Christian Case for Land Reform

ROY H. MAY, JR.

ORBIS BOOKS

Maryknoll, New York 10545

OCLC: 22387648

The Catholic Foreign Mission Society of America (Maryknoll) recruits and trains people for overseas missionary service. Through Orbis Books, Maryknoll aims to foster the international dialogue that is essential to mission. The books published, however, reflect the opinions of their authors and are not meant to represent the official position of the society.

Copyright © 1991 by Roy H. May, Jr.

Published in the United States of America by Orbis Books, Maryknoll, New York 10545

An earlier Spanish version of this book, *Los Pobres de la Tierra*, was published by Editorial DEI, Apartado 390-2070, Sabanilla, San José, Costa Rica (© 1986 by DEI). The present text has been thoroughly revised.

Unless noted otherwise, biblical quotations are taken from the Revised Standard Version.

Manuscript editor: William E. Jerman

Library of Congress Cataloging-in-Publication Data

May, Roy H.
    [Pobres de la tierra. English]
    The poor of the land: a Christian case for land reform / Roy H. May, Jr.
        p.   cm.
    Rev. translation of: Los pobres de la tierra.
    Includes bibliographical references.
    ISBN 0-88344-729-0
    1. Land tenure — Religious aspects — Christianity.   2. Land reform — Latin America.   3. Liberation theology.   4. Latin America — Church history.   I. Title.
    BR115.L23M2413   1991
    261.8'5 — dc20   90-46980
                                                                                          CIP

The Poor of the Land

For Janet, Richard, and Robert

Contents

Preface

The unjust distribution of land and the rapacious assaults by the powerful on the lands of the poor are fundamental causes of poverty and misery in Latin America. Land can be an important hermeneutic for understanding contemporary Latin America, because it is such a central politico-economic theme. Indeed, in one way or another, nearly all social injustice can be traced to land—who owns it and how it is used. Even urban problems are integrally connected to land. Not only are the millions of migrants pouring into Latin American cities those who have been expelled from the countryside, but upon arrival in the city there is no space available to establish a home. So they live in the streets or build cardboard and tin shacks on precarious hillsides and over polluted rivers, one on top of the other. Control of land means power, and that power is used without pity against the poor.

Land also is a central theme in the biblical tradition. The moving force in the history of ancient Israel as recorded in the Hebrew Bible is the struggle to obtain, and then to maintain, "promised land." The same theme is taken up by Jesus as a salvific symbol for the poor. It is through the concept of land that eschatological hope takes historic form.

In the midst of the critical Latin American situation, it is urgent that the church rediscover that biblical tradition of land, understood now in its contemporary socio-historical context, in order to define a mission of solidarity with the victims of land injustice. For peasants, small farmers, and Amerindians, as in the biblical tradition, land continues to be the historic symbol of salvation. It is important that the church incarnate that hope in its mission praxis.

The title of this book, *The Poor of the Land*, points to the landless and exploited rural poor. They are the campesinos, the small farmers, the Amerindians, the rural workers, the day laborers, the drifters—in short, the exploited, marginated populations that serve powerful economic interests and are being pushed aside as countries strive for "modernization" and "development."

The title also recalls an important but often overlooked biblical image that points to the same people. From 2 Kings (25:12) and Jeremiah (39:10) we know that when Israel was sent into exile, the poorest were purposefully left behind. They were the "poor of the land" (Amos 8:4), those forced off their properties, whose livestock was stolen by powerful economic interests (Job 24:2–4), those "trampled upon" (Amos 8:4), and "thrust off the road" (Job 24:2–4) by powerful estate owners. They were the ones left to be exploited by Israel's conquerors as agricultural day laborers, as peons on the great estates (2 Kings 25:12). The title is most appropriate, for they are still the "trampled upon."

This book is about land and the poor in Latin America. Originally published in Spanish and then in Portuguese, its basic purpose was to contribute to the Latin American church's consciousness of the "poor of the land," and of the problem of land as a critical justice and mission priority. It grew out of my own pastoral experience among Amerindian peasants in the highlands of Bolivia. Land is a major concern of theirs, and they wanted to know what the church and the Bible had to say about it. A year in Central America introduced me to the transnational reality of Latin American agriculture and what that meant for the poor and their land. So I began working on the theme, not only to put together my own thoughts, but also to provide resources useful to others in Latin America concerned for the poor of the land.

It is evident, however, that the problem of land in Latin America cannot be reduced only to internal factors, as important as they may be. Land injustice in Latin America is related integrally to a whole complex of international economic and political relationships in which the United States plays a key and dominant role. It is important, therefore, that the concerns of this book be shared with First World persons who also are concerned for justice in Latin America. This is the fundamental reason for publishing this revised version in English.

Land injustice is not only a Latin American and Third World concern; it is a North American concern. A few years ago during a brief period teaching at Saint Paul School of Theology in Kansas City, Missouri, a group of professors and students spent a weekend in southern Iowa, one of the hardest hit farm crisis areas in the United States. We stayed with farm families and listened to their stories. I was struck by the similarity of what struggling, middle-class Iowa farmers told me about their situation, and my own experience among Latin American peasants. One evening my host family asked about the crisis in Central America. I told them about landlessness and debt. Suddenly they understood what was going on in Central America.

Indeed in the United States major corporations increasingly are monopolizing not only the commercialization of farm produce, but even the fundamental resource itself — land. High production costs benefiting the major agricultural products suppliers, increased indebtedness benefiting the banks, and monoculture production benefiting seed suppliers, agrichemical companies, and large commercial houses increasingly marginalize independent, family farmers. Industry invests in small, rural towns to spark "rural revitalization" by providing jobs to losing farmers — but at minimum wages and no unions. As in Latin America, farmers forced off their land provide a pool of exploitable, cheap labor. Iowa farmers can understand Latin America.

During that same time in the United States, my family and I vacationed in the Black Hills. We returned to Kansas City across southern South Dakota, across the Pine Ridge and Rose Bud Sioux Indian reservations. Beside the mass grave of Sioux Indians massacred by the U.S. Army at Wounded Knee in 1890, I spoke with several young Amerindians. Their story also is the story of the struggle for land.

So although this book is about land in Latin America, I hope it will speak to those who are concerned deeply for justice in the land in the United States. Perhaps the Latin American experience and therefore this book is not "transferable," but I hope it will provide insight into the U.S. reality. Above all, I hope the book might contribute toward the solidarity of all those in the Americas who are struggling for justice in the land.

There are, of course, various ways to approach the theme of the land. For example, not only the socio-political situation but native cultures also offer rich and profound possibilities. The traditions of the Pachamama of Andean cultures, and of the "Land without Evil" or the "Holy Mountain" of Amazonia, understand the land as part of the essence of life. Thus they suggest deep possibilities for theological reflection. Likewise the natural order and ecological wholeness suggest a theology and spirituality of the land. My text does not develop these possibilities, although these approaches are recognized. Rather, my approach is decidedly political and economic, because I believe these are the fundamental issues that first must be understood and resolved. This is the approach that also has primarily characterized the Latin American church's concern for land.

This political and economic concern is evident throughout the book, especially in the first two chapters where the problem of land and its economic rationale in Latin America are presented as fundamental justice themes. There is no attempt to present a complete panorama, country by country, of the problem of land. Instead, countries I know best are presented as representative examples of the Latin American reality.

Chapter 3 discusses the biblical tradition of land understood in the Latin American peasant context. The purpose is to demonstrate that land is not only a fundamental biblical theme, but also has much to say to the peasant struggle for land in contemporary Latin America. That biblical history is not alien to Latin American history; rather, it is the same history of the poor of the land even today.

The last three chapters emerge from the first ones. Chapter 4 presents an overview of the Latin American church's concern for land, and the emergence during the 1980s of what it calls "ministry from the land" as a new pastoral mode. The chapter looks particularly at the various pastoral letters on land that were published during the decade, and emphasizes the letter of the Guatemalan bishops and the public response to it. Chapter

5 focuses on Brazil. It is in Brazil where the church has taken land most seriously, and it is there that the concept of "ministry from the land" emerged.

Finally chapter 6, a more theological and pastoral reflection, attempts to trace concrete guides for solidarity with the struggle for land in Latin America. The brief Epilogue simply puts the problem of land, and therefore the church's mission, in a perspective greater than just Latin America, because land is the problem of the poor throughout the world.

I hope, then, that these words stimulate a more systematic reflection, and, above all, that they will move the church toward a serious mission practice in favor of land justice. At the 500th anniversary of Columbus's voyage to the Americas and the subsequent invasion and evangelization of native cultures all in the name of God and land, the church can wait no longer to place itself unequivocally on the side of the poor of the land.

The Poor of the Land

TESTIMONY

''I am Conchita, the Squatter''

Between 1985 and early 1989, the Pavones de Golfito region in southern Costa Rica, on the Pacific coast, was the scene of intense conflict among peasant squatters, North American landowners, and the Rural Assistance Guard. This is the testimony of one of the squatters.

My name is Concepción Rosales, but since I was little I've been called "Conchita." I am 32 years old; I'm the mother of six children and I'm pregnant. I'm a peasant born in Guanacaste (in northern Costa Rica) and since two years ago I'm a squatter in Pavones de Golfito.

I was born in Nandayure. Later my dad went to work for the banana company [United Brands], and so we all went to Golfito; he was the only one of us working. When he died my family and I went to Puñta Zancudo. I was 14 and so I began working the land. Since then that's my world.

When I was 15, I met Luís Angel Porras and married him. His family was from Pavones. We left Zancudo for Pueblo Nuevo de Coto, and then to Pavones. We worked on the farm of Alejandro Gómez, and bought a piece of land.

My husband went to pan gold at Puerto Jiménez and one day, five years ago, a tree fell on him and a companion, killing them

1

both. I couldn't see him because he had been dead three days before I was told.

My oldest son, Mainor, was 14 and didn't want to stay on our little farm. We sold what we had in La Hierba de Pavones and went near the beach.

I was happy with my husband but now I was left alone. I decided to fight for a piece of land for my children and became a squatter; since then I've been thrown off the land, mistreated, and I've been in jail.

The first time that the Rural Assistance Guard came to my little house I was scared, because I'd never been in these things. But as time went by, I became accustomed to it all. Now I'm not afraid of them even though they burn my little house and destroy what I've planted. I'm not afraid now because the hope of having a little piece of land for my children and me gives me strength.

They've thrown me off seven times. The only time I was saved in these two years was in April last year.

Now last December 9, the Guard came and I was with my companion (I started living with him a year-and-a-half ago), and was with my children. I cried more for the hunger they would feel if they were carried off, than for me. I know what it means to be in jail.

They took us that Friday and it wasn't until Saturday night that they gave us something to eat. They took us from Golfito to San Isidro and again to Golfito. They sent me to the Buen Pastor Jail, and I got out today.

For me, jail has been hard because I don't know anything about my children. I believe they are with my sister-in-law who lives in Pavones. When I've been detained, I've been treated good and bad. Don Beita, of the Golfito police, doesn't let me make telephone calls and so I don't know anything about my children.

In the Buen Pastor Jail, the girls behave themselves well, but I feel sorry for the little guilas ("kids"). I have six children: Mainor, 17, Meylin who's going to be 15, Amixia, 12, Luis Iván, 10, Ana Doris, 8, and Jenny Luisa who's almost 5.

In Golfito the government agency for children has told me that if I continue being a squatter, they'll take my little kids, and that I'll never see them again, and that they'll send me to Buen Pastor Jail. That worries me, but I keep on going. I want a piece of land and even though a lot of people tell me to get off, they're not going to give me or my children anything to eat.

Those of us here at Pavones are going to keep on; the struggle ends when the Lobo family and others leave us the land that they don't cultivate. My ambition is to have land even if it's just a little plot to leave my children. It's better to live in the country than here in the city.

Aportés, March 1989, San José, Costa Rica.
Used by permission. Translation mine.

CHAPTER 1

Land and Justice
in Latin America

For five hundred years, ever since Columbus arrived in the New World, land has been the basis for greed and power, giving rise to the tragic disjunctures of power, of rich and poor throughout Latin America. Quite simply, ownership and control of land determines who lives and who dies. The process, spurred on by "development and modernization," has increased significantly in the last three decades. The result has been the genocide of whole peoples, the expulsion of millions of campesinos from their lands, forcing them to become part of Latin America's massive urbanization, and the subjection and exploitation of those who remain on the land as a cheap source of labor for the powerful.

By the turn of the century, 75 percent of Latin America's population will live in cities. Such rapid urbanization, however, hides Latin America's essentially rural orientation. With at least 100 million persons living at or below the subsistence level, 65 percent are rural. Of these, 50 to 70 percent are landless or nearly landless. Depending on the country, 40 to 70 percent of the economically active population are engaged in agricultural work, and agricultural exports represent between 35 and 85 percent of Latin America's total exports, with national averages being around 65 percent. Throughout Latin America, the highest levels of infant mortality and illiteracy, and the lowest levels of income and life expectancy, are in rural areas. Even though there has been a relative decrease in rural population vis-à-vis the cities, the past thirty years have witnessed an absolute population increase. The fact is there are more persons than ever living in the countryside.[1]

LAND AND THE STRUCTURE OF POWER

Land long has been the decisive factor in Latin America's political economy, because its ownership and control has meant power and domination over the principal means of production. The longtime fundamental character of Latin American agrarian structure is the concentration of huge extensions of land, latifundios, providing for a very small minority of the local population. The majority is landless or reduced to extremely small landholdings. Thus today 7 percent of the population owns 93.8 percent of the land.[2] This extreme concentration of land is even greater than statistics show, because frequently a single landowner or his family will own several large estates.

The roots of this agrarian structure are in the Conquest and the subsequent development of the hacienda and plantation.

In the colonial and republican periods, the hacienda, or great landed estate, developed on the basis of a monopoly of land and water, and the domination of a servile, peasant population. The system was closed, based on the exploitation of not only cheap, but free, labor. Although production had ties to external, even international markets, it was oriented primarily toward the hacienda's own needs and that of the immediate area. Technologically conservative and making few investments for increased productivity, the landlord made his fortune exploiting labor. The hacienda often became a small kingdom in itself, dominating the surrounding area, and manifesting itself as a semifeudal system. The estate's servile peasant population received in usufruct tiny parcels of land for personal use, but between the small size of the holdings and the amount of time demanded in personal and labor services to the landlord and his family, the peasant's share was reduced to a minimum. Thus the contradiction between landed and landless was established. It would become the foundation for power even in contemporary times.

At the same time, in the humid coastal and tropical areas, a plantation economy arose, based first on sugar cane and later on tropical fruits. These plantations were originally worked by slaves. Following emancipation, planters employed large numbers of workers, often their ex-slaves, also under conditions of exploitation. Out of that system arose a whole class of landless or nearly landless rural workers, sometimes as a rural proletariat, often as sharecroppers and day laborers, all totally dependent on the company or grower. The plantation, as today, was closely aligned with the international market and dependent on foreign capital and market demands.

Faced with the hacienda and the plantation, peasants and Amerindians found it increasingly difficult to maintain lands and control over their own labor and production. Many Amerindians were exterminated, as in Argentina and Brazil. Peasants were incorporated into the hacienda, as in Mexico, Guatemala, Peru, and Bolivia:

> After the end of the colonial epoch, the local white or mestizo elite in most of the Latin American countries expanded its wealth and power in an aggressive way, mainly at the cost of the indigenous peasants. Thus, the process of pushing back the indigenous peasant population towards more remote and even more barren agricultural areas was initiated.[3]

This process reached its apex, however, in the republican period. With the arrival of the liberals and their ideals of individualism and private property, the expulsion of Amerindians and peasants from their lands had philosophical blessing. In the colonial period the Spanish Crown at least attempted a measure of protection for Amerindian rights. The Amerindians paid tribute — in money or labor — to retain their land rights. The republicans, however, changed that. For them, the Amerindians were occupying lands that belonged to the state and therefore rightfully could be expelled for greater national interests. It was this philosophical and legal concept that opened the way for liberal attempts at the wholesale expropriation of Amerindian communal lands. Therefore republican governments refused to recognize communal lands, the basis for indigenous social-economic organization, and by force and in the name of liberty, imposed a system of private property. The liberals arbitrarily divided communal land among the Amerindians and then took the "surplus land" as state property to be sold to creole landlords. Thus in Mexico in 1856 collective landholdings were prohibited, and twenty years later private land companies were given the right to take "titleless land." In El Salvador, *ejidos* or communal property was abolished in 1882.

In Bolivia, in 1866 and 1868, General Melgarejo decreed "the reversion in favor of the state of all so-called original and community lands for sale in public auction." He violently enforced the decrees, driving at least 300,000 Amerindians from their properties and handing over the "vacant lands" to eager landowners. In 1874 the *Ley de Exvinculación*:

> proposed the definitive extinction of the *ayllus* [communal lands], the privatization of tenancy and the creation of a land market that would permit the formation of great agricultural properties. Remaining marginalized from the agricultural market, these "primitive" forms of social organization would finally be eliminated.[4]

Toned by social Darwinism, the *Ley de Exvinculación* purposely sought the destruction of "the hybrid and pernicious system of [indigenous] communities," as a cabinet minister said in 1889. Although many Amerindian communities already had productive farms and a highly developed commercial system, the law, in the words of an official report:

> [was to] bring out of stagnation great territorial values and jerk a whole race out of its semi-savage state in order to cultivate it and convert it into an element of national property.[5]

For liberals, civilization was identified with commerce, and their civilizing and self-serving mission was justified because the

Amerindians were inferior, semisavages. They did not believe in the *private* ownership of land.

In Bolivia the process of expelling Amerindians from their lands continued well into the twentieth century. Half the haciendas expropriated following the 1953 land reform were formed after 1880.

Throughout Latin America, campesinos and Amerindians resisted the taking of their lands. So tenacious were they that the conquistadores and then the republicans seldom were able to completely dominate the land or completely impose their liberal projects. Still, uprisings were brutally suffocated, every time with loss of life and land.

The large estate, owned by the Spanish and Portuguese landlord, came to dominate rural Latin America. As Ernest Feder writes, "The *latifundio* has been and continues being an oppressive and arbitrary form of agriculture."[6] From this agrarian history the large landowner emerged as an extremely powerful figure, integrally woven into the whole socio-political and economic fabric. Again as Feder explains, "In a *latifundio* agriculture, landlord harshness is institutionalized."[7]

Under modern capitalism, however, the large landowner is no longer the conservative, rural aristocrat. He is an urban, progressive capitalist, involved in many different enterprises, part of a new agrarian bourgeoisie:

> Although the economic, social and above all the political power of the landed elite is land-based, their major interests are not necessarily agriculture. A high proportion of politicians, lawyers, doctors, merchants, farm equipment dealers, owners of transportation (trucking) businesses, exporters, importers and even industrialists are also owners of large sections of farmland.[8]

Indeed, their principal interests may not be agriculture at all. Often these "new landowners" take advantage of their agricultural and livestock properties primarily as tax shelters and for other financial benefits that can be transferred to other businesses, or as investments for future land speculation and capital needs. Still, they have great power, not only through control of land and various other business enterprises, but also because of their relationship to international capital and manipulative access to their own nation's political structure.

THE CONTEMPORARY SITUATION OF LANDLESSNESS

In spite of land reforms and the rural development programs launched over the last thirty years, the situation of campesinos, small farmers, and Amerindians[9] has deteriorated to the point that their survival as distinct social sectors is questionable. Their situation is worse than in 1965 when the Alliance for Progress, the massive U.S. aid program that was supposed to bring justice and development to the countryside, was beginning. Rural injustice and inequity are increasing.

In Mexico the number of landless peasant farmers has increased ten times since 1950, until today there are more than fourteen million people—half the rural population—without land of their own. Some five million farm workers are employed less than 90 days a year, and land occupations have increased significantly since 1975.[10]

Guatemala has one of the most unjust land tenure systems in Latin America. Some 88 percent of the farms have less than seven hectares each (one hectare = 2.5 acres), and occupy only 16 percent of the farmland; 9 percent have 45 hectares and occupy 19 percent of the farmland. Only 3 percent are big farms, but have 65 percent of the agricultural land. These figures do not indicate the thousands of peasant farmers who have no land at all. In El Salvador, 29 percent of peasants did not have land in 1971; 41 percent were landless in 1975; and by 1980, 65 percent were landless. In Honduras, 68 percent of all the country's farmers have less than three hectares each, occupying only 12 percent of agricultural land. On the other hand, less than one percent of agricultural properties appropriate 20 percent of the land, each estate averaging 1,800 hectares. Perhaps 85 percent of all farmers are landless. It is hardly surprising that, according to a survey, 75 percent of Honduran peasants would be willing to participate in a land occupation or "invasion."

The Costa Rican situation is similar. About 85 percent of the nation's farmers control less than a quarter of the land. At least

20,000 peasant families are landless. Between 30 and 35 percent of all farms are worked by farmers who do not own them.[11] Much of the land is owned by foreigners or foreign-owned corporations. The situation is desperate for most of Costa Rica's small farmers. As a farmer in the Guanacaste Province said, "We have to get rid of our land or make radical changes in our way of working." In the same region an agronomist working with small farmers explained:

> The situation is very difficult. With rising costs and lower prices [for agricultural products] the small farmer can't compete with the big ones. The big guys are going to buy the land of the little ones, and they will then have to work as laborers for those who bought their land.

A study of Costa Rica's small farmers concludes:

> The prognosis for the peasant is not good. Options have evaporated and no sign of relief is in sight. . . . The Costa Rican countryside of the future is likely to see the almost complete disappearance of the remaining small-farm peasants, for they will be unable to compete with the industrial giants.[12]

In South America one finds the same phenomenon. The average Bolivian farm in the heavily populated Lake Titicaca region has only 3.2 hectares, and 80 percent of the area's farms are less than five hectares. Many persons have access to only a few furrows. Landlessness has been a growing problem for the past thirty years. Many highland farmers have migrated to the eastern lowlands where various Bolivian governments have offered 30 to 50 hectares free. However, these colonization or new lands development programs have been difficult at best and have suffered high rates of land abandonment. Instead, large landholdings have come to dominate. Nearly 99 percent of the rich agricultural lowlands is concentrated in estates from 500 to over 10,000 hectares.[13] Overall, 93 percent of Bolivia's landowners are small farmers, with only 11 percent of the agricultural land at their disposal.[14]

Although Brazil is "an agricultural superpower second only to the United States" in terms of agricultural export earnings, the small farmer hardly benefits.[15] Half of Brazil's farms have less than 10 hectares and occupy barely 3 percent of the agricultural land; nearly 40 percent of the farmers have no land at all.[16] Just under one percent of the farms, however, make up nearly 43 percent of all agricultural properties, while 90 percent of all agricultural properties are limited to 21 percent of the land. In the north and central west, 70 percent of agricultural properties have over 1,000 hectares,[17] and estates surpassing 100,000 hectares are common in Mato Grosso and Amazonia where small farmers also are struggling to get a piece of land. In the late 1970s, 141 properties alone held 30.6 million hectares, or 10 percent of Brazil's agricultural land. In the impoverished northeast, small farms represent nearly 80 percent of the region's farms, but occupy barely 20 percent of the land area. In thirty years, the number of "squatter farmers" increased from 95,867 to 511,052.[18] On the other hand, large estates, only 1.5 percent of the total farms, control 35 percent of the land.[19] Thousands of northeast farmers are landless, making their living as tenant farmers, sharecroppers, and day laborers on the great estates, and as sugar cane cutters on the plantations. Throughout Brazil, especially since 1964, empirical data clearly show a strong tendency toward extreme concentration of land, thus widening the gap between landed and landless.

These statistics are illustrative of the trend toward land concentration throughout Latin America. However, they do not show how a single family or company often owns various estates. Nor do they explain that the small farmer's land is nearly always of marginal quality. Likewise they do not reveal the great number of mechanisms available to landowners and companies for maintaining political and economic control that in turn assure their domination of land. But these too are factors that gravely affect peasant farmers.

The accelerated changes occurring in Latin American agriculture as reflected in land tenure patterns under the pressure of modern capitalism show that significant new socio-political relationships are emerging. The owners of the great estates are emerging as a new agrarian bourgeoisie, allied with international capital and closely related to urban industrial and financial interests. At the same time, the traditional peasantry is more and more "de-peasantized" in that it can no longer make a living off the land, turning into a semiproletariat that must sell part of its labor to the new capitalists, or, finally, leaving all independent agricultural production to become genuine proletarians completely dependent on company wages. In all cases the uprooting of peasants and small farmers means the availability of a large supply of cheap labor for the new capitalists. How social class structure is being affected and reconstituted is debated. But changes are occurring and those changes do not bode well for the poor of the land.

LAND AND AMERINDIANS

"The elimination of all but a few Amazon tribes by the year 2000 is all but inevitable," an anthropologist has observed. Confronted by capitalism's insatiable appetite for land and its wealth, Amerindians suffer more than anyone else. The invasion of their traditional lands by ranchers, miners, lumbermen, agro-industrialists, speculators, colonists, and others, means, at best, permanent changes in their way of life, and at worst, their physical extinction, a true genocide. Sadly this is not a situation peculiar to a single country, but common to all.

Control of land is the fundamental issue. Amerindians are often hunters and gatherers, roaming over continuous geographical territories, with only intermittent and dispersed agriculture. Within those territories they develop economic and existential needs. Territory and cultural identity tend to be inseparable. Their land is understood as an integral whole of territory and natural resources that forms the psychophysical base for their livelihood. To take their land is to take their lives. Even as their cultures evolve in the direction of peasant society, through contact with Western society, tribals continue to exploit forest resources for their economic well-being. However, they do not have legal (state-given) titles, and the concept of "territory" seldom is part of a nation's legal codes. Thus tribal lands are easy prey for developers.

With its immense tropical forests and expanded plains, rich

in natural resources, the situation of Amerindians is especially acute in Brazil. Since 1900 more than a million Amerindians have died, reducing the indigenous population to less than 300,000. Eighty-seven different Amerindian groups have been exterminated. The situation has been particularly grave since the 1960s when Brazil's ruling generals decided to develop the Amazon. "Indigenous people are harassed constantly; all possible means are used to subjugate and exterminate them," according to a study of their situation.[20] Their lands are invaded for cattle ranches, mining, and lumber interests. During the 1960s and early 1970s, the policy was that of extermination. Thousands died of diseases contracted from whites pouring into their territories over the transamazon highway system.[21] Whole villages were massacred from the ground and from the air with dynamite and machine guns. Measles and tuberculosis were introduced deliberately, along with sugar laced with arsenic, and other similar measures, to exterminate Amerindian communities.

If genocide was not official government policy, the military government was guilty through complicity, for it did nothing to stop the extermination of tribals or to protect their rights and interests. Even when territories were designated, they were not respected. As Shelton Davis concludes in his well-known work, *The Victims of the Miracle*:

> The Brazilian government, in other words, could have intervened to protect these Amerindian land areas against outside encroachments, and could have planned highway and development projects so as not to have threatened the territorial integrity of Amerindian tribes. . . .
>
> Between 1970 and 1974, Brazilian Indian policy became increasingly compromised with the larger economic development policies of the Brazilian military regime. During this period, the Brazilian national Indian Foundation became a chief accomplice in the processes of ethnocide that were unleashed on the Indian tribes of the Amazon Basin. Its "reformed" Indian policy, to state the situation most simply, tended to speed up, rather than stop, the

processes of ethnic destruction that have so bitterly characterized the frontier history of Brazil.[22]

During the late 1970s and early 1980s, because of international pressure and internal changes within the military regime that finally gave way to civilian, democratic government in late 1984, the practice of killing Amerindians as a *policy* ended. Instead policy shifted to settlement, incorporation, and even recognition. The government began to talk about how Amerindians would benefit from development projects through jobs when they lost their land. An Amerindian was elected to congress, and others were allowed to participate in the direction of FUNAI (Brazilian Amerindian Foundation). But FUNAI was decentralized and stripped of its power to demarcate Amerindian lands, and Amerindians were declared children before the law, incapable of handling their own affairs—but adult enough to be workers. The struggle for their lands remains as difficult as ever. At the end of the 1980s, less than 4 percent of Amerindian lands have been legalized. Meanwhile increasing numbers of Amerindians again are being murdered as gold prospectors and others flood the far reaches of the Amazon basin. With the Amazon's mineral wealth estimated at some $100 billion—30 to 40 percent of it under Amerindian lands—the attitude expressed some time ago by a former governor of Roraima characterizes the situation that Amerindians face: "I think that [with] an area so rich in gold, diamonds and uranium, the luxury of saving a half-dozen Amerindian tribes that are blocking the development of Brazil cannot be permitted."[23]

Although he wrote several years ago, Davis's conclusions still are valid:

There is nothing inevitable about what is taking place in the Brazilian Amazon. Nor are there any compelling reasons for believing that the Amazon development program will benefit the vast majority of the people of Brazil. The silent war being waged against the people and environment of the Amazon Basin is the result of a very specific "model of development."[24]

Pushed by its enormous foreign debt, everything is justified in the name of development and within that "specific model" private monopoly of land by large corporations and private wealthy individuals is the key.

A WORSENING SITUATION

For the poor of the land the situation is worsening. They increasingly are dispossessed of their lands and prohibited access to new lands because of (1) large-scale, commercial agriculture; (2) cattle ranching; (3) dams and water resource development; (4) mining and petroleum production; and (5) ecological destruction.

Commercial agriculture, with its almost exclusive export orientation, is capital intensive, requiring rationalization and efficiency, often under the control of transnational agribusiness. As financial incentives (profits) increase, more and more pressures are exerted against the landholdings of small farmers and peasants as commercial farmers seek to expand the size of their landholdings for increased production. Small farmers cannot compete. They do not have land or capital. Under conditions of high costs ("modern technology") and low prices for their traditional ("nonexport") products, only with difficulty can they resist pressures on their land (if they are the owners) and their cheap labor. Commercial agriculture squeezes them out, even marginalizing their labor as mechanization increases. Marketing processes encourage farm consolidation into larger units. It is cheaper to buy in bulk from a few large producers than to buy the same amount from a large number of dispersed small farms. Thus expansion is encouraged but at the cost of the small producer.[25] Agricultural wealth increasingly is concentrated with the new agrarian bourgeoisie and its ties to transnational agribusiness.

This process, in various forms, can be seen throughout Latin America. In Costa Rica, for example, favoring commercial agriculture for export, the main thrust of agricultural policy since the 1960s, has had central importance in the 1980s. Agricultural diversification has attempted to move the country away from total dependency on coffee and bananas, to new plantation crops such as cacao, citrus fruits, pineapples, palm tree products, even casava for the Hispanic market in the United States. Flowers and ornamental plants are accorded special importance. Particularly in the Atlantic coast region, new estates of 400 to 800 hectares, owned by agribusiness concerns often backed (or owned) by transnational capital, increasingly have dominated. The result is a strong tendency toward further concentration of landholdings.

Increasingly commercialization also is responsible for greater landlessness in Brazil, particularly the northeast. Market incentives for sugar cane production, due to Brazil's decision to use alcohol for energy, caused tremendous expansion of land area planted in sugar cane. Tenant farmers were pushed off the land they cultivated, and small holders were pressured into selling. Again the result was increased concentration of landholdings and greater landlessness.

Cattle ranching is a similar process implying the monopolization of land. As the profitability of beef for export rises, ranchers pressure the lands of small farms to turn them into pasture, or expand into new areas often already claimed by poor squatters. This has been notable throughout Central America. In the 1960s in Costa Rica, with loans from the World Bank and the Inter-American Development Bank (IDB), beef production increased dramatically, but at the cost of the continual dispossession of small farms. Guanacaste Province, once dominated by small farms, increasingly has been oriented toward ranching, with the consequent monopolization of land by the new cattlemen, thus changing the character of the entire region. The small farmer has had to go elsewhere. In Guatemala, especially in the northern regions of Alta Verapaz and El Petén, as well as along the western coastal plain, ranchers continue to have peasants cut the forests to make way for pastures.

Furthermore, with its low labor requirements, expanded beef production negatively affects employment. Ranching does not absorb into its labor force the small farmers who lose their land to pastures, nor does it create new employment possibilities.

Ranching also often is a "cover" for land speculation and capitalization for other industries. This can be seen in north-central Brazil, in the states of Pará and Mato Grosso along the

Araguaia River. This region, called the "Polo Pêcuario Xingu-Araguaia," originally was the territory of various Amerindian tribes but now is dominated by ranches ranging in size from 100,000 to 500,000 and more hectares. The owners are automobile and liquid gas companies, banks, government officials, and transnational enterprises with various interests.[26] The extremely ample fiscal incentives and subsidies[27] offered by the Brazilian government have been a source of capitalization of São Paulo industries, through the transfer of capital available for ranching to urban industries, as well as tax shelters for other business endeavors. Profits are "invested" in ranching and therefore are not taxed. At the same time the monopoly of such huge tracts of land has made speculation an extremely lucrative business, or at least provides a hedge for future capital needs.

In the case of Brazil, ranching has meant the decimation of Amerindian tribes,[28] and, as in Costa Rica, the uprooting of traditional small farmers. Cattle ranching may put beef on the tables of the rich world, but it hardly benefits the poor of the land in Latin America.

Water resource development is another way that small farmers and Amerindians lose land. What should be evident immediately is that reservoirs take a lot of land. What perhaps is not so evident is that the poor of the land seldom benefit from irrigation and energy generation.

In the 1970s the development of hydroelectric resources became a major component of Brazil's development plans. Construction began on numerous large dams across some of Brazil's biggest rivers, creating huge, artificial lakes. They hardly have benefited peasants and Amerindians.

The most ambitious hydroelectric project ever undertaken in the world is the Itaipú Dam across the Paraná River dividing Brazil and Paraguay. Begun in 1973 and opened eleven years later, the new lake flooded 1,400 square kilometers of land. In Brazil thousands of small farmers, many with well-established market ties, were displaced. Land values increased significantly, attracting speculators. Agribusiness interests, already pressuring the area's small farmers, also increased. So serious has the situation become for small holders that they have launched the *Movimento dos Trabalhadores Rurais Sem Terra* (Movement of

Landless Rural Workers), nationwide in scope but with its origin and primary strength in southern Brazil.

The situation may be worse on the Paraguayan side. Many of the Brazilians who lost land on their side have moved across the river into Paraguay as colonists. With rising land values stimulated by the dam and colonization, land companies have moved in, and agribusiness concerns, many foreign-owned, especially by Brazilians, also have come, developing an easy working relationship with the area's traditional large landowners. The Paraguayan government, once the owner of large tracts of land in the area, has sold off most of its holdings at cut-rate prices to high-ranking military officers and officials of the ruling Colorado Party. They in turn have sold the land at market prices to land companies who have resold it to wealthy farmers and agribusinesses. In all, small farmers and Amerindians have gained little. In fact, they have lost land.[29]

In 1978 the Sobradinho Dam on the São Francisco River in Brazil's northeast was completed. The hydroelectric complex provides energy for sugar mills and, especially, the petro-chemical industry. The 4,214 square kilometer reservoir, however, forced 50,000 people from their lands. Most were small, subsistence producers with weak market ties.[30] The Tucurui Reservoir, on the Tocantins River in the state of Pará, began filling in 1984. It too would expel several thousand from their land in order to generate electricity for the gigantic Carajás mining project. Especially affected were the lands of various Amerindian tribes. Damming its huge Amazon Basin rivers continues to be a major component of Brazilian development. Plan 2010 will construct 105 hydroelectric plants and flood 30,400 square kilometers of land. At least 250,000 people, nearly 30,000 of them Amerindians, will be displaced.

Hydroelectric projects may provide energy for the rich, but they take land from the poor. Of course such projects also often are justified by their potential for irrigation, theoretically available to rich and poor alike. However, irrigation tends to favor the wealthier and to encourage land consolidation. Irrigation water seldom is free, and installations are costly; thus the wealthier farmers have an immediate advantage over poorer ones. Also, since large-scale irrigation systems are cheaper and more efficient when utilized on larger land units, land consolidation is stimulated. At the same time, irrigation increases the value of land, making land speculation an attractive business opportunity. Over all, water resource development tends to work against the land's poor.

The development of mineral resources is another way the poor, especially Amerindians, lose land. In Latin America mineral resources usually belong to the state, following the old Spanish and Portuguese law that gave mineral wealth to the Crown. The state grants exploration and exploitation concessions independent of who lives on the land. Mining and petroleum production often signify large tracts of land controlled by the private or state companies that exploit the buried resources. Seldom is there compensation or benefits through royalty payments for those who live there if they are Amerindians or poor farmers.

By presidential decree in 1983, Brazil opened Amerindian reserves and other traditional Amerindian territories for mineral exploitation by private individuals and companies. Thousands of gold prospectors flooded Indian reserves. Although the 1988 Constitution cancelled the decree, many hundreds continue to prospect rivers and mineral deposits. However, mineral interests already were responsible for decimating Amerindian populations. Highways leading to potential mineral deposits had poked into the remotest regions of Amazonia, "opening" Amerindian lands and in the process carrying deadly diseases. At least one attempt had been made to wipe out a whole tribe in order to gain access to the area's mineral wealth.[31] Independent gold prospectors already had invaded lands, especially in the central west. The Amazon region hides one of the richest and most diverse mineral deposits in the world. Brazil clearly is bent on "developing" it, human cost aside.

One of the most ambitious mining projects is the Carajás Project in the north-central states of Maranhão, Pará, and northern Goiás. The multibillion-dollar program will exploit iron, copper, gold, aluminum, manganese, nickel, and tin, at various sites throughout the region. Contracts have been given to Brazilian and foreign companies, with 80 to 100 percent of mineral production destined for the world market.[32] The vast project will displace thousands of small landholders, and affect the territories of numerous Amerindian tribals. The best they can hope for are jobs.

Finally, ecological destruction, related to all that has been discussed here, is another way the poor lose land. The rural poor cannot move on when the soil is eroded and worn out, nor can they quit jobs that force them to work in fields freshly sprayed with agrichemicals. When the forests are gone, Amerindians have no place to go nor the means to continue their way of life. Soil erosion, deforestation, and the indiscriminate use of agrichemicals are the principal forms of ecological destruction affecting Latin America's rural poor.

At least 39 percent of Bolivian soils are eroded seriously, with the most affected areas being the Altiplano and Andean valleys. These are the areas of Bolivia's traditional *minifundistas* or Amerindian peasant farmers. Years ago mining and railroad companies cut what timber grew on the Altiplano and virtually nothing has been done to restore soil and water resources. Today these depleted soils are one reason Amerindian peasants eke out only a subsistence living.

Throughout tropical Latin America, deforestation is causing still unknown damage to the natural environment. No place is this more evident than in Brazil. Literally thousands of hectares of rain forest have been cut by lumber companies and ranchers. At the present rate of cutting, the Amazon rain forest will disappear within two generations. Aside from still unknown effects such deforestation may have on hydrological systems and microclimates, the destruction of the tropical forest threatens the very existence of Amerindian tribals. Their way of life is a symbiotic relationship with the forest, in delicate but perfect ecological balance. To destroy the forest is to destroy them.[33]

The indiscriminate use of agrichemicals not only affects the health of the poor of the land, but also destroys their land. In Costa Rica the worn-out lands of a banana company were bought as part of the nation's land reform to be distributed to small farmers who had lost land in other parts of the country. However, residues of chemical fertilizers remaining in the soil interfere with the maturation process of rice, thus making the small farmers' "new land" almost worthless as agricultural property. Injury to farm workers due to agrichemicals is reported from all across Latin America. Neurological disorders, sterility, blindness, birth defects, even deaths, have become commonplace among Latin American agricultural workers.

Clearly the consequences of ecological destruction are suffered first and most by the poor of the land. They are the ones left holding the bag. The rich move on, but the poor must stay.

LABOR RELATIONS AND LANDLESSNESS

Landlessness is intimately related to agricultural labor relations. Growing landlessness assures a growing and permanent force of cheap labor whose insecure relation to the land makes it easily exploitable, keeping wages at barely subsistence levels, and union organization weak. As modern capitalist agriculture has advanced, the number of rural wage earners has increased dramatically. But most of the work is seasonal and contracts are vague and unwritten.

The exploitation of labor by large landowners hardly is new. The Spanish conquerors developed it into a fine art through the *mita* and *encomienda*, and the subjugation of Amerindians as serfs on semifeudal estates. The republicans refined the hacienda and used vagrancy laws to force Amerindians to work for large landowners. Laws also were passed that required Amerindians to work up to a hundred days a year on the large estates.

Today tenant farmers and sharecroppers not only are subject to the production requirements of the landowner, but also contribute considerable amounts of free labor in return for land. Wages are paid irregularly and then only at subsistence levels.

Each year in Bolivia, as a consequence of landlessness or near landlessness, 25,000 peasant farmers migrate from the highlands to join at least an equal number of year-round agricultural workers in the eastern lowlands to harvest cotton and sugar cane. Nearly 80 percent of those migrating from the highlands own less than five hectares, and over a third own fewer than two hectares. The resident agricultural labor force is entirely landless, living on the edges of large agricultural estates or in the marginal neighborhoods of Santa Cruz, Montero, and other cities and towns.

Most are recruited by labor contractors who prowl the highlands advertising the money-making possibilities as seasonal harvesters, promising benefits that never materialize. Ninety-nine percent never have written contracts, and are paid in cash without any written records. Usually they are paid at the end of the harvest, based on the amount of sugar cane or cotton harvested. They work eleven-hour days in actual harvesting, gathering, weighing, loading, and transporting the cane and cotton. However, only harvesting is remunerated; the other activities are free labor contributions to the grower. Payment is approximately one dollar a day; a family of four might earn three dollars daily. Since 1984 temporary agricultural workers have been included in Bolivia's General Labor Law. The law, however, has proved to be no more than a piece of paper. Labor union organization has strengthened the position of temporary workers, but most remain unorganized.[34]

Temporary and seasonal rural labor is an institutionalized part of Brazil's agrarian structure. There, *peonaje* is modern slavery.

The labor demands for clearing the thousands of hectares of jungle dedicated to pastures for the immense cattle ranches in Mato Grosso and Pará have required hundreds of thousands of day laborers (*peones*) and landless farmers from the northeast and other parts who come seeking work. They are hired by a labor contractor[35] who, for a set fee, has agreed to supply a ranch with a certain number of laborers. He pays the laborer's outstanding bills and then transports him and others to the ranch. The contractor and the ranch manager, however, deduct all these costs, including room and board, sometimes even rent for ranch-supplied housing, from the laborer's salary. At the end of the work period, the laborer often receives nothing. If during the work period the laborer wishes to leave, the ranch's hired gunslingers stop him. If he "escapes," they hunt him down, often with the help of the Federal Police, and bring him back. He has "debts" to pay off. In the Polo Pêcuario Xingu-Araguaia such debt-*peonaje* is the common practice.[36]

In areas that grow sugar cane, citrus fruits, and vegetables a whole class of agricultural day laborers — *bôias-frias* ("cold lunches") — has emerged. They live in urban shantytowns, leaving each morning at four or five, traveling in the back of a truck to begin harvesting crops at seven. Most are women, children, and teenagers. They return home at night after having earned less than a subsistence day's wage.

Union organization among agricultural workers and small farmers and peasants generally is weak. Not only does the temporary character of their work and geographical dispersion hinder organization, governments do too. In Mexico and Brazil unions are organized and controlled by the government. Severe restrictions are placed on the right to strike and "closed shop" union contracts are prohibited. Combativeness is discouraged by requiring that unions provide social services, thus attracting members more interested in services than strikes. Legal blocks make the organization of confederations or nationwide associations difficult. Many times unions themselves are divided, with two or three groups vying for control. Seldom are agricultural workers and peasants united with urban industrial workers. Sometimes they are even pitted against each other.

There are important exceptions, however. In spite of legal obstacles, Brazil's sugar cane cutters are militantly organized and have won important concessions from growers. Unions of peasants and other small holders are demonstrating increasing independence and militancy. Even unorganized *bôias-frias* have gained concessions after street rioting protesting poor wages, labor conditions, and hunger. In other areas of Latin America there have been unprecedented strikes by agricultural workers. Bolivia is one of the best cases. There, nearly three million peasant farmers are united into a single confederation, which in turn is integrated into the Bolivian Labor Center (COB). In recent years the confederation's militancy has been demonstrated on more than one occasion by massively blockading the nation's highways. Concessions have included better prices for their products and incorporating migrant harvesters into the General Labor Law, providing social and legal benefits.

The poor of the land always have resisted. Outbursts of violence and revolutionary movements, refusal to accept new technologies, and maintenance of ancestral traditions are some of the ways that resistance has been expressed. Always latent, it continually will be expressed in new forms as new circumstances are met.

LAND REFORM

Nearly all Latin American countries have had some kind of land reform. Some (in Mexico, Bolivia, Cuba, and Nicaragua) were the result of revolutionary situations. However, most land reforms occurred in the 1960s as planned agrarian policy pressured by the Alliance for Progress, with little intention of restructuring power. With the exception of Cuba, no land reform has dealt decisively with the issues of rural justice discussed in this chapter. At best, they have been "indecisive."[37]

Monopolization of agricultural land by 22 large sugar companies (13 of them U.S.-owned), and by other big growers in the face of a mass of landless or near landless peasant farmers, was a principal cause of the Cuban revolution. Especially in the Sierra Maestra, peasants participated in the armed movement. Following the revolutionary victory in 1959, restructuring land tenancy and improving the lot of small farmers and rural workers became central concerns of the revolutionary government. "Ruralism" became an ideological slogan and agriculture was designated the leading sector for economic transformation.

Initially, the new government decreed that large (400 hectares or more), inefficient or underutilized farms would be expropriated for their redistribution to land-poor farmers, and a "vital minimum" size (27 hectares) was established as a standard for individual holdings. Completely landless farmers were organized into cooperatives. However, nearly a year later only six thousand families actually had benefited. Between 1960 and 1962, the government nationalized many foreign agricultural enterprises as well as large, Cuban-owned agribusinesses. By mid-1961 the government controlled just under half the nation's farmland. Cooperatives were redesigned as state farms, and the central government assumed the principal role in agricultural ownership and production. In October 1963 a "second agrarian reform" was enacted that reduced the minimum landholding subject to expropriation to only 67 hectares, thus further weakening well-established landowners. Today agricultural planning and production are centralized in the state. A private, small farmer or peasant sector continues to have a role in agricultural production, but most rural cultivators are government employees on state-owned enterprises.[38]

Without question the Mexican revolution and its land reform brought about dramatic changes in agrarian structure and rural social relations. However, as many have observed:

> The Mexican agrarian reform, consolidated in the constitution of 1917 but fruit of a long period of peasant rebellion, eliminated the old latifundist structure and profoundly changed the peasants' servile relation to the traditional *haciendas*. The new social, political, and economic structures permitted the gradual formations of one of the most coherent bourgeoisies in Latin America, although essentially dependent, in this case aggravated by the proximity to the U.S.[39]

By 1970 there were as many landless farmers in Mexico as there were at the beginning of the Mexican revolution. In 1910, 66 percent of the rural population was landless; today the figure stands at about half the rural population. Even with restrictions, Mexican agrarian policy consistently has favored commercial agriculture with transnational ties. Recent agrarian legislation gives even fewer guarantees to small holders, opening the Mexican countryside even more to commercial interests.

The most significant achievement of land reform in Bolivia was to dramatically alter social relations. Peasants were freed from their serflike condition.

Changes in land tenure were less spectacular. The 1953 land reform did expropriate the large Altiplano and Andean valley estates, but simply legalized the individual plots that peasant farmers already held in usufruct. In some cases, land reform meant a reduction of land the peasant had, and at best signified only small increases, never surpassing 25 percent of what the peasant already had. The result was to legitimize small holdings and accentuate the extreme fragmentation of scattered land holdings.[40]

At the same time, agrarian policy was oriented toward creating a viable agro-industry in the country's eastern lowlands. Agro-industrial complexes increasingly dominate, displacing small farmers who have come to the area as "colonists" in new land development schemes. Much of the concentration of land occurred during the 1970s military regime of General Hugo Banzer who manipulated the national land reform agency to reward loyal cronies.

The same land reform patterns can be seen throughout Latin America. In Peru, the agrarian law emphasizes agro-industrial development, ignoring the mountain regions where peasants represent 61 percent of the nation's farmers. The far-reaching 1969 land reform law degenerated into bureaucratic and top-down administration, frustrating what might have been something new among Latin American land reforms. Colombia's 1960s land reform "did not modify the land-holding structure of the country, on the contrary, it strengthened and accelerated the capitalist development process in favor of the large landholders."[41]

The Central American experience is similar. In Honduras land reform functions only under heavy peasant pressures, and land that is distributed tends to be of marginal quality. In Honduras, if peasants want fertile land, they have to take it. Indeed without the strategy of land occupations, the effectiveness of Honduran land reform is questionable. Costa Rica's land program often is upheld as a model. Yet small farmers as a class are disappearing, pressured by large, commercial estates and agribusinesses. At the same time that Costa Rica says it wishes to provide land for poor farmers, it focuses on a policy of commercial export agriculture that emphasizes land consolidation. Indeed part of land reform is to take care of farmers expelled from their lands in other parts! This is particularly evident in the southern region where the government has obtained banana company land for redistribution to farmers who lost their land to ranchers in the northern Guanacaste Province. As one study concludes, "the political will for realizing an agrarian reform does not exist at the highest levels of decision-making."[42]

On paper the 1980 El Salvadoran land reform was far-reaching: all properties over 500 hectares were to be expropriated and turned into cooperative farms; medium-sized agricultural estates (100-500 hectares) would have been confiscated and divided among small producers; rented, share-cropped, and squatter-claimed lands were to become the property of the "tiller." In practice, however, land reform has been less significant.

Although the large estates were expropriated, only 15 percent of the nation's farmland was affected. The great bulk of wealthy farms, including important coffee, cotton, and sugar lands, fall within the medium-sized category. They remain untouched; the land reform provisions affecting them have never been implemented. The third phase — "land to the tiller" — finally has benefited nearly 65,000 peasant families, representing about a quarter of the rural poor.

El Salvadoran ruling elites have resented and strongly resisted even the idea of land reform. Only because of extremely heavy U.S. pressure was land reform enacted, and only then as an effort to preempt the revolutionary movement and to lure peasants to the government's side. In carrying it out, the military has been accorded the central role, thus turning land reform into an instrument for greater government control of the countryside and means of repression. Hundreds of peasant land reform activists have been murdered and cooperatives turned into government and military centers. Finally, many beneficiaries of the "land to the tiller" phase have abandoned or sold their lands due to intimidation and forced eviction by former owners.

Over all, land reform has been subject to intense political jockeying and changes within the El Salvadoran government, the military's need to defeat the armed movement, and the elite's desire to maintain economic power. That the poor need land to survive is hardly a consideration.[43]

The Nicaraguan experience stands apart from the rest of Central America, although not without ambiguities. Indeed, it is a case study of the difficulties of land reform within a revolutionary context in which democracy and pluralism remain ideological commitments.

Peasants were the backbone of the Sandinista revolution and promised land was their central motivation. Upon taking power in 1979, the Sandinistas expropriated the extensive holdings of Somoza and his associates, thus obtaining at one stroke 23 percent of the nation's agricultural land, including about fifteen hundred modern, commercial farms. Not only did the expropriation give the new government a great deal of land for redistribution, it also encountered little opposition from the agricultural upper class — also fed up with Somoza.

Eager to maintain high levels of agricultural production, most of the land and modern estates were established as state farms. Although credits granted poor farmers were greatly increased, rents significantly lowered, and idle and long-rented land turned over to the user-producer, only a minimum of land actually was redistributed among land-poor peasants. Rather, this first phase (1979–83) of land reform sought to consolidate the state sector and to avoid conflict with the well-established producers.

The second phase (1983–85) emphasized cooperatives, not only for providing crucial support services, but also for agricultural production. Peasant discontent due to the minimal distribution of land during the first phase was now evident, and the government responded by organizing hundreds of poor farmers into cooperatives, and by legalizing the lands of thousands of individual peasants. Still, however, massive redistribution of confiscated farmland was not part of the Sandinista program. The government continued to be concerned for high levels of agricultural production, not only for export but especially for the domestic food supply. It also was concerned to assure adequate labor resources for the export sector.

Important material benefits were gained. Agricultural production increased and domestic food supplies were strengthened. (Although by the mid-1980s the gains began to erode due to adverse weather conditions, and especially, the U.S. sponsored war against the Sandinista revolution.) Political benefits were less satisfactory. The agricultural bourgeoisie and other wealthy social sectors escalated their scathing accusations of wholesale expropriations and human rights abuses by the Sandinista government. Peasant discontent, channeled through their strong organizations, continued to be evident.

During 1984 grassroots peasant pressure began to impact significantly the nation's land reform. Their demand was for individually owned land. Grants to individuals in 1985 increased ten times over the previous year; some state farms were broken up and turned over to peasants; the government increased purchases of large estates. Titling continued at a faster pace. In 1985–86, more land was distributed to individual peasants than during the entire period since the revolutionary triumph.

Certainly land reform has meant significant changes in Nicaragua. Land tenancy has been restructured and new forms of land ownership and production introduced. By the mid-1980s, two-fifths of the farmland had been obtained by the government and mostly divided into state farms and cooperatives. By 1987, only 61 percent of the land was in individual or private holdings, and large farms represented only 10 percent of the nation's agricultural estates. Still, private property is guaranteed and most government land acquisitions have been through purchases, rather than expropriations. Efficient producers, regardless of size, are protected from confiscation. Overall, at least 83,000 peasant families have benefited.

Nevertheless, neither the wealthy agricultural upper class nor the poor peasants have been entirely satisfied. The Sandinista government continually found itself in a difficult policy-making situation as it sought to respond both to economic needs and to conflicting political demands, all in the context of a counterrevolutionary war and economic embargo against it. In 1985 the Central American Historical Institute, a Managua-based agency, reported that the dilemma of land reform was "how to develop an agrarian policy which promotes national unity, maintains the guarantees made to the private sector, and regains the support of the peasants." The 1990 electoral defeat of the Sandinista government suggests that the dilemma never was resolved satisfactorily, and that the future of land reform in Nicaragua remains a critical question.[44]

Land reform in Latin America has not dealt with the unjust structure of power. There are two reasons for this. One is that land reforms are not directed toward changing that structure, but rather preserving it by co-opting pressures against it. The second reason is related to the first. Land reform is an instrument to stimulate commercial agriculture. There nearly always is a significant loophole: only nonproductive land is redistributed. Thus by putting land into production—for example, by introducing cattle—landowners can keep their large holdings, or at least keep the best land, giving only marginal land to landless farmers. Feder calls this *"a new concept of social justice for the landed elite*, i.e., that it is unjust to expropriate land which is more utilized."[45] In other words, the issue is not justice for the poor; if the rich use their land, it is okay for them to retain it — even if it means keeping the masses landless. At bottom the unequal distribution of land and the power that inequality confers have not been concerns of land reform.

LAND AND VIOLENCE

The highly unequal distribution of land and participation in the benefits of agricultural development are the source of considerable violence. At times it has surfaced in revolutionary movements as in Mexico in the early part of the century, and more recently in El Salvador and Guatemala.

Indeed, there is a correlation between violent conflicts and pressures on peasant lands, particularly when peasants are squeezed off their traditional farms or expelled from new, untitled lands they claim as squatters.[46] Even under the best of circumstances, the economic situation of peasants is precarious. When their economic or material situation deteriorates to such a degree that they cannot provide for their basic needs, they tend to rebel. Land, of course, is the material key to their capacity to reproduce their basic needs.

In Guatemala the areas of violence include not only traditional peasant areas characterized by the small holdings and landlessness. They also include new lands that peasants have claimed as squatters, but which are coveted by the wealthy for cattle ranching and mineral production. At the end of the 1970s and the early part of the 1980s, these areas witnessed unprecedented violence against the civilian, peasant population when the armed forces declared war on peasants in order to end the guerrilla movement and to assure themselves control of land. Several massacres are directly attributable to the desire of the military and the wealthy for land claimed by Amerindians.[47] In El Salvador, statistics demonstrate that guerrrilla activity coincides with a period of rapid land loss by peasants. It is not by chance that the areas dominated by the revolutionary forces are peasant strongholds.

Usually, however, violence is not revolutionary violence but rather the violence of greed by large landowners and agribusinesses who seek to expand their holdings and maintain intact the rural power structure now with its urban connections. That violence is constant and institutionalized. The forcible expulsion of small holders from their lands, and the murder of rural union leaders who organize resistance, is part of the rural scene in Paraguay, Mexico, Brazil, and other countries. As Feder explains, large landowners and agribusiness concerns maintain a private police force.

> They make the workers "toe the line" through intimidation, terrorization, and corporal punishment. At times they kill. These "policemen" prevent workers from joining unions or peasant leagues by threatening those who become actual union leaders. They contribute a great deal to the violent conflicts between workers and administration, and cases of brutality arise frequently.[48]

Nowhere is this system of violence against small landholders and rural workers more evident than in Brazil. Since 1964, over fifteen hundred rural workers, squatters, Amerindians, peasants, priests and religious workers, lawyers, ecologists, and others have been murdered in land-related conflicts. In a two-year period in the mid-1980s, some five hundred people were murdered. At the end of the decade, in one year alone over one million people were involved in 715 disputes over land that left 153 people dead. Most of the victims were rural labor union leaders and the victimizers the private police of growers.[49]

In the cattle ranching central-west, the pattern of violence continues. Thousands of landless farmers have gone to the region seeking land and have established small farms, usually without legal title, although Brazilian law recognizes the right to possession after a year and a day. Large landowners, now organized into the Rural Democratic Union (UDR), backed by government policy and sometimes titles given in Brasilia without anyone ever having visited and surveyed the tract of land, claim the same land for their ever-expanding empires.

Following the system described by Feder, hundreds of private gunslingers, *jagunços*, are hired by UDR landowners to expel the *posseiros*, the small holders who already are farming the land or who simply move in on the large, idle sections of the estate. Cattle are stampeded through the *posseiro*'s crops; paths to his property are fenced. Finally his house is burned, his family is threatened, and, if he refuses to give in, he is murdered.

The authors of this violence, although publicly known (the Catholic Church's Pastoral Land Commission even publishes their names), seldom are arrested and never tried. Less than a dozen cases have ever been before Brazilian courts. They act with impunity, with the complicity of the federal police and government agencies.[50] Indeed, they utilize the bureaucratic-military apparatus in order to impede access to land by the poor, thus generating tragic conflicts among people, government, and social classes.

As the Pastoral Land Commission explains:

These conflicts of interest align, on the one hand, the *hacienda* owners, the large landholders and the swindlers, who are fighting to maintain and perpetuate the actual situation, that is to their benefit. On the other hand the squatters, small landholders, sharecroppers and hired hands are fighting to defend the right to have a piece of land on which to survive.

The position of some of defense of privileges and the struggle of others for the conquest of their rights is defined by the Brazilian agricultural structure, a structure which tends to monopolize and concentrate land holdings. Those who are affected by this violence (the squatters, small landowners, sharecroppers and hired hands) react. But their reaction, until now, has never been as violent as what they have suffered. It is barely a defense of their rights, a defense that, a majority of the time, fails to materialize because they are crushed by the stronger and more powerful ones.[51]

Violence is a tragic reality growing out of the unequal distribution of land and power, aggravated by official policies that perpetuate injustice. Violence means power and domination, and its victims are the poor of the land.

CONCLUSION

Latin American agriculture is being converted into a grand commercial enterprise that forms part of an internationalized agro-industrial complex. In the process a new class of modern capitalist landlords is being created, only reinforcing the old inequalities of social class and facilitating expulsion, often violently, of peasants, small farmers, and Amerindians from their lands. The small holders cannot compete; they have no resources; they cannot absorb the risks. Little by little they die on their tiny plots, or leave by the thousands for the cities of São Paulo, Lima, Bogotá, San José, Tegucigalpa, or Mexico City, simply "working around" day after day, without future, without hope.

This chapter largely has been descriptive of the Latin American situation of landlessness. In the next chapter I will try to analyze some of the underlying theory that causes and attempts to justify landlessness.

CHAPTER 2

Development Theory
and Landlessness

Neither chance nor fate is responsible for the Latin American rural reality. It is, rather, the result of carefully designed policies that obey a particular model of economic development emphasized especially since 1950. International development agencies have played a key role in imposing this model. Much of its planning, implementing, and resourcing are attributable to the Alliance for Progress and the U.S. Agency for International Development (AID), the International Bank for Reconstruction and Development (World Bank), and the International Monetary Fund (IMF). Now with the debt crisis, these institutions have pushed even harder for adjustments in the economies of Latin American nations to conform more fully with their concept of development, a concept clearly in the interests of the capitalist powers. Within their model of development, the processes described in the first chapter are seen not only as logical consequences, but necessary in order to achieve a modern, developed society. In this chapter I will explore that economic development model and its relationship to landlessness.

THE CAPITALIST ECONOMIC GROWTH MODEL

The capitalist economic growth model that dominates Latin America's struggle for development understands growth and modernization as the keys to development. Within the logic of that model, modernization means the transformation of so-called primitive and traditional sectors into a capitalist, market-oriented and technology-based economy for sustained economic growth or expansion. Economic growth itself is understood as the aggregate expansion of the economy. The distribution of economic growth among social sectors seldom is considered important and often thought impossible. In fact, many economists believe that concentration of growth—or wealth—is necessary in order to achieve high levels of capital accumulation and rates of savings that in turn will be invested in modern industry (including industrialized agriculture). The fundamental concern is economic growth.

Capital accumulation and savings for investment and market expansion are seen as crucial elements to achieve the continued expansion of the economy. Savings—that is, money left over after buying basic needs and desired luxuries—are particularly important because they are the source of investment. Savings make the economy grow. However, since domestic savings or money that a nation itself "saves" or makes available for investment are small, at least in comparison to investment needs, foreign contributions or investments also are desired in order to augment domestic savings and therefore investment capacity. According to the model, the poor cannot save, but the rich can. Hence, economic policies must favor the rich. At the same time international loans and transnational corporations are important "foreign contributors" to savings and investments. They also are important sources of modern technology and means for market expansion. Both are crucial to growth. Without market expansion, investment is meaningless, and without cost and labor-reducing technology, growth is impossible.

THE SPECIAL ROLE OF AGRICULTURE

Agriculture has a special role as a supplier of "surplus labor" to industry, and as a source of foreign exchange.

According to the economic growth model, thousands and thousands of campesinos and small farmers are underemployed in agriculture and therefore can be transferred to productive employment in urban industry and industrialized agriculture. As long as they remain in agriculture, they are only unproductive "surplus labor," contributing nothing to growth. In industry, including agro-industry, however, they become productive contributors to economic growth. They also contribute to domestic savings because they can be hired for subsistence wages plus a little more as incentive to leave traditional agriculture. What they are not paid is their contribution to domestic savings. They are a cheap, industrial reserve labor force, virtually unlimited, ever-ready for an expanding capitalist sector.

This is seen clearly in the case of Guatemala. The extremely skewed land tenure system, with its enormous imbalance between minifundio and latifundio, serves well the labor needs of those who dominate the national economy. Landlessness and near landlessness produce thousands of peasant farmers who must sell their labor in order to survive. Their great numbers and precarious economic situation force down wages and keep union organizing weak. But there are other benefits for the landed class. Not only does the system assure a steady supply of cheap labor, it also contributes in other ways to the capital accumulation of the wealthy. With the introduction of cattle and the expansion of lands dedicated to nontraditional products, there is a great need to cut the forest and open new lands for pasture and export agriculture. When landless peasants from the highlands rent parcels of forest or brushland on the coastal plain or in the northern regions, they not only have to pay rent in money. In addition to the plots they work for their own needs, the peasants must clear a certain amount of land and seed it for pasture. The following year the peasant might return to the same estate, but cannot return to the same plot as the year before. Instead he must move to another area to perform the same labor tasks for the owner. Thus, the land is prepared at no cost to the landlord. Rather, the peasant pays the owner for the right to work!

Agriculture especially is seen as a means for quickly generating foreign exchange. The "law of comparative advantage" says that a nation should produce those products that other countries cannot, or that it can produce more cheaply or "efficiently" than someone else. This can be for geographical and technical considerations, labor costs, and many other reasons. By focusing production on high demand export products, such as beef, tropical fruit, and flowers and other ornamental plants, for which it has a "comparative advantage," a poor country can ease significantly its chronic balance of payments problem, earning badly needed foreign exchange. Thus the growth model also is highly oriented toward export production. The small market, it is believed, also dictates that orientation.

THE MEANING OF DEVELOPMENT

Agricultural development, then, is a function of the economic growth model and agriculture's special role within it. The basic goal is to increase agricultural production ("growth") for increased savings. Since it is believed that small landholders are unable to save, and since small size is believed to be inefficient, land consolidation is a necessary development strategy. At the same time, mechanization, modern technology, and "innovation" must be introduced, for they are believed to be requirements for increased production. They also are most efficient on larger holdings.

According to the model, agro-industry,[1] especially transnational corporations, is a necessary component of agricultural development. It supplies investment capital, technical capacity, and market arrangements. It also supplies inputs and efficiency through the integration of production, processing, and distribution systems.

Rural development schemes are designed to facilitate this kind of agricultural change. The World Bank and Inter-American Development Bank pour millions of dollars into infrastructure projects: roads, hydroelectric plants for energy and irrigation, transportation systems, and the like. All kinds of technical improvements (mechanization, chemical fertilizers, "green revolution" seeds, land reclamation) are introduced. Land reform is encouraged for modernization and increased production. Social services such as health and educational facilities are introduced to improve the quality of labor and to ease the social disjunctures that development often implies, and to buy support for development programs. Development agencies are created as means of socio-economic control, and to assure a more effective governmental presence in rural areas. There is wide variety in how such programs are effected, who does them, and how the various social sectors benefit. Some approaches are far more humanitarian and concerned with the poor of the land than others. Nevertheless, "rural development" nearly always is the agent for putting into practice the economic growth model of development.

CONTRADICTIONS IN THE GROWTH MODEL

As a result of the growth model, various Latin American nations have increased significantly their agricultural production. Mexico, Colombia, and Brazil, even tiny Costa Rica, have become great exporters of agricultural products. Yet, as we have seen, since "development" began in each of these countries, landlessness has increased and the disparity between rich and poor has widened. This is seen in Mexico, a nation often cited as a positive example of agricultural development, where the bulk of agricultural income is concentrated among only five percent of Mexican farmers. Mexico, Brazil, and Costa Rica, in spite of agricultural growth and participation in the world market, are food deficit countries, all having had to import in recent years basic food stuffs, including the basic staple, black beans.

In each of these countries concomitant with agricultural development has been increasing penetration and control over production, processing, and distribution systems by transnational agro-industries and further concentration of economic power in a new agrarian bourgeoisie with its diversified interests in "modern industry." The growth model's emphasis on aggregate growth simply means the rich get richer, and the poor poorer.

Likewise, the growth model, with its concept of "surplus labor" whose "marginal productivity is zero," is responsible for massive unemployment and landlessness as peasants and other small holders are squeezed off their land by "modern" agriculture and industry. At the same time, unlike the theory, this "surplus labor" is unable to find new work in urban industry, but, like the theory, does keep wages low for those few who do find new work. The model transfers peasants to the city, but does not transform them into workers. The massive "urban problems" of Latin American cities are manifestations of the growth model of agricultural development.

Finally, with the growth model, food production declines severely. As we have seen with Mexico, Brazil, and Costa Rica, export orientation does not produce food crops, especially basic staples, for national consumption. Everywhere food is produced primarily on small farms. In Costa Rica farms of less than 50 hectares produce between 22 and 29 of the nation's basic food crops, including vegetables, beans, and corn.[2] In Brazil farms of 10 hectares or less produce over 80 percent of the nation's beans, 90 percent of its cassava (mandioca), and 70 percent of home consumption corn.[3] In Bolivia, minifundists produce 70 percent of the corn that is cultivated in the country, 85 percent of the rice, 100 percent of the barley, 80 percent of the wheat, and 100 percent of the potatoes, in addition to vegetables and fruits.[4] Similar figures can be cited for all of Latin America. Simply put, the anti-small farm bias of the growth model is a major cause of hunger. "Economy of scale" tends to create a homogeneous export-oriented agriculture highly dependent on the international market and companies, almost always to the detriment of food for the table.

This, however, is not contrary to the development model. Indeed, food production is not the purpose of agriculture. Rather, the purpose of agriculture is to produce *income* for families and the nation. As a well-known agricultural economist writes:

> Families and nations can have enough to eat if they have sufficient income, no matter how that income is earned. Food can be purchased, and it can be imported if it is not produced in sufficient quantities and variety domestically.[5]

Following the law of comparative advantage, a country should import those products someone else can produce more cheaply. Since, for instance, Costa Rica does not produce corn, beans, and rice as "efficiently" as the highly technicized and subsidized U.S. farmer, economic theory dictates that Costa Rica import those products rather than produce them. That is exactly what Costa Rican economic policy is doing. Pressured by AID, the World Bank, and the International Monetary Fund, Costa Rica has made the policy decision not to produce basic grains. Rather those basic products are to be imported from the USA. By refusing credit and price supports to corn and bean farmers — peasants — Costa Rica is effectively marginalizing domestic food producers from agriculture. Instead, the government urges them to participate in the "agriculture of change" geared exclusively to the export of tropical fruits, nuts, flowers, and similar products that they are not in condition to produce.

If the results of the growth model are contradictory for human welfare, it also contains theoretical flaws. In the first place, "growth" can be distributed or stimulated in the poorest rather than the richest sectors. Economic expansion does not have to be concentrated among an elite. Given investment policies and other income-raising strategies favoring the lowest economic sectors, growth can be stimulated among the poor, thus substantially altering income distribution within one or two decades.[6]

Although studies are not numerous, empirical evidence suggests that the so-called surplus labor is not surplus at all. Rather it is necessary to maintain actual levels of production. Certainly labor productivity is low and underutilized, but to transfer the "surplus" causes production to decline.[7] Gunnar Myrdal, stating flatly "that the marginal productivity of labor is zero is factually incorrect as well as theoretically invalid,"[8] argues instead that yields are low because of the underutilization of labor and therefore that "an increase of the labor input — achieved by improving participation ratios, and the duration and efficiency of work — would raise yields even without any technological innovation or additional investment, except work."[9]

There also is ample evidence attesting to the efficiency of small farms. In fact, small farms are more productive — efficient — per hectare than large farms, and make important contributions to the national economy.[10] In Bolivia, minifundist agriculture annually contributes some $500 million to the national economy. It also can use and benefit from technology. Finally, given the opportunity and incentive to do so, peasant farmers also are willing to adopt new and improved farming methods.[11]

In addition to its empirical contradictions and theoretical flaws, the capitalist growth model of development is based on a seriously erroneous assumption, that of a "dual" economy, one "traditional" and the other "modern," as the basic hermeneutic for understanding rural reality.

THE FALLACY OF THE DUAL ECONOMY

According to the dual economy assumption, the "traditional" sector is backward, conservative, and irrational (because it does not maximize profits), and represents the masses of poor farmers. The "modern" sector, on the other hand, is progressive and capitalist. Although small, as the economy's "leading sector" it is ready to innovate and expand. It is assumed that the modern sector is the motor for development, and that development's goal is to transform the traditional sector into the modern sector.

At best this assumption is only a description of appearance. In reality there are no "dual" sectors. Rather the double appearance is the expression of a single economy characterized by exploitation and domination. The concept of "traditional" is based on a preconceived notion of peasant society as a static, cultural type, somehow divorced from socio-historical reality.

POLITICAL ECONOMY OF PEASANTS

Little understood is that peasant societies exhibit characteristics of a specific mode of production that has been called "peasant economy,"[12] and that has been shaped first by Latin America's history of semifeudalism and more recently by agrarian capitalism.

Peasant economy is characterized by the following:

(1) Production in the first instance is motivated by, and oriented toward, the family unit, seldom above the subsistence level, concerned with producing basic needs.

(2) Only in the second instance is production oriented toward the market. Market ties are weak, and the peasant producers never generate capital from the sale of their products. Whatever

surplus they produce always is transferred under very unequal terms of exchange to the dominant social class. The major concern is not accumulation, but rather distribution within the family and community.

(3) Labor is not hired but contributed by the family itself and the village community through various forms of mutual assistance and collective endeavors. On the other hand, peasants often must sell or contribute their labor to the dominant economic interests.

(4) Land is the basis of their livelihood. Nevertheless land is never understood as private property in the capitalist sense, but as family property or community property. (The fact that many peasants are landless and must rent or share-crop represents the decomposition of peasant economy before the dominant economy.)

(5) Existential identification is with the family, the family property, and village in such a way that the individual, family, and village community form an indivisible whole.

(6) The basic organizational structure/control over land resources is the village.

Although these six characteristics represent an ideal type, and over the years with increasing capitalist penetration have become eroded and distorted, they still can be observed in various forms throughout the Latin American countryside.

Certainly for understanding the political economy of peasants,[13] analysis must begin with "peasant economy" and focus on three primary levels: the family, the village, and the state, all within the context of capitalist socio-economic and political structure. The family is the major source of personal protection. The village serves as a buffer between the family and the state. The state, "controlled by central elites endowed with authority, wealth, status, education, and coercive power," is the means for expropriating peasant production and resources.[14] In Bolivia the state often plays a key role in keeping peasants poor. For instance, when the price of potatoes has risen, the various governments often have imported potatoes from Argentina in order to keep the price of potatoes at or below production costs.

Peasant economy, then, must be understood within the social, economic, and political conditions and constraints the dominant social class has determined.[15] That is, peasant societies, isolated from a total system, cannot be understood. For centuries that system has been characterized by domination and exploitation of peasants — the "traditional" sector — by a more powerful socio-economic class, the "modern" sector. In other words, as we saw in the case of Guatemala, the dominant social class always has had a vested interest in creating the so-called traditional sector as a source of cheap labor and cheap land, the principal factors of agricultural production.

Given this socio-historic matrix, peasant economy is a rational response to protect self-interest against a hegemonic social class that seeks to exploit peasants. Thus peasant economy endeavors to locate control of land use and resources, as well as socio-political organization, within its own trusted social group. Likewise an exploitive market is avoided as far as possible by producing almost exclusively for the family and village. At the same time, by relying upon family and community labor, peasants try to control their own labor resources, at least as far as self-needs are concerned. Traditional conservatism is a means of maintaining personal and class integrity, of resistance to being subordinated to the capitalist class. As one author explains:

> The resistance of peasant producers is manifested in a number of ways: refusal to adopt new cultivation practices or their sabotage — thus peasant conservatism — bearing in mind that such measures introduce further elements of risk in the already precarious material basis of household production; peasant strikes involving the refusal to grow certain crops or cutting back on their production, that is, attempts to withdraw, at least partially, from commodity relations or to find alternative sources of cash income (e.g., labor migration); evasion of crop-grading regulations and of the terms of exchange imposed by state or other monopolistic agencies of merchant's capital — by smuggling and other forms of illicit marketing in order to realize a higher return to labor; as well as political actions, including individual or collective acts of violence, against agents of capital and state functionaries in the rural areas.[16]

Characterizing peasants as backward and irrational hardly is appropriate. In fact, what analysis demonstrates is that peasant economy is highly successful, not at enriching, but certainly at caring for basic human needs for survival in the face of often overwhelming odds. In this sense the peasantry is a nation's strength, not a draw-back.[17]

However, the capitalist growth model of development intentionally destroys peasant economy. As one observer has noted, deeming peasants as backward has been a "charter for all sorts of intervention"[18] in favor of the dominant capitalist class. The growth model says the "traditional" sector must be transformed into the "modern" sector. What happens, though, is that the "traditional" sector is not transformed but transferred out of the countryside or to big commercial operations as cheap laborers. "Traditional" and "modern" are two expressions of a single system — traditional being the exploited and dominated, modern the exploiters and dominators. Both have emerged because of differing relationships to capital.

NEEDED CHANGES IN THE DEVELOPMENT MODEL

A fundamentally new development model giving priority to the poorest rural sectors is needed if the poor of the land are to have a just and secure economic base. The contradictions in the growth model that have been discussed in this chapter are suggestive of some of the new directions the model must take. The new model must respect and build upon peasant economy, and facilitate small producers through policies of investment and enhancement of their savings capacity. The domestic market for food production will need to be emphasized and, under conditions of a market economy, the terms of exchange must be weighted in favor of peasant farmers. Labor saving, but not labor replacing, technology must be introduced for more efficient utilization of labor for increased yields.

However, the new model also must move toward the socialization of factors of production and agricultural inputs and other resources. At least in areas of acute land shortage, the collective ownership and use of land will be necessary. Likewise, the nationalization of plantations and large agricultural estates and ranching enterprises will be required for worker management or ownership. At the same time agricultural support systems, such as mechanization and technical and financial inputs, will need to be collectivized.

Certainly independent, class-based organizations, such as unions and peasants leagues, must be stimulated. Only through aggressive, grassroots organization to confront the dominant class interests will changes in favor of the poor of the land be possible.

Fundamental, of course, is land reform that is not only a redistribution of land, but is a radical restructuring of power. Without this kind of land reform there is little possibility of achieving justice and well-being for the poor of the land. Without the transfer of power to them, changes are unlikely. In reality, genuine land reform cannot be separated from transformations that must occur throughout the entire society. In this sense, land reform must be part of a global process of social structural change. Only within that context will land reform signify genuine changes. That is, for instance, what makes Nicaraguan land reform under the Sandinista government truly significant. As suggested earlier, the land reform law itself hardly is radical. Yet inserted in the total revolutionary process it meant profound changes.[19]

DEVELOPMENT AS A POLITICAL PROCESS

When we discuss the poor of the land as investment priorities in order to achieve a fundamental redistribution of wealth and income, or of land reform as a radical restructuring of power, it is obvious we are discussing political decisions. It is not a question of growth; it is a question of where growth occurs and who benefits. That is an entirely political question.

At bottom, development cannot be understood mainly in economic and technical terms.[20] Development must be understood in political terms, as the struggle of the poor of the land for new structures governing socio-economic relationships. The causes of poverty and underdevelopment are politico-economic structures of inequality and exploitation that are encrusted in Latin American nations and reinforced by the international order.

Structures are institutionalized sets of relationships within a society. They may be formal or informal, but they bear on the quality of life of social classes because they determine who has access to the nation's supply of wealth and services. Powerful groups monopolize wealth and services for themselves, excluding and exploiting weaker groups. Unless these unjust relationships are transformed radically, efforts to improve the quality of life for the poorest will be ineffective.

This means development may involve conflict, again underlining the political nature of development. Historical experience demonstrates that powerful elites seldom give in (or give up) easily. Social reform and equitable distribution of wealth and power always have been won through hard-fought struggles. This does not necessarily imply "revolutionary violence," but it does mean the poor of the land standing together to confront those who would deny them the basic necessities of life.

CONCLUSION

Pushed by the debt crisis of the 1980s, Latin American countries are incorporating as never before the economic growth model with its antipeasant bias, creating landlessness and poverty instead of the promised prosperity. However, the effects of the economic growth model hardly are limited to Latin America. They are felt throughout the Third World with the same consequences for the poor of the land. Pressured by the ever-increasing indebtedness of the countries, the economic growth model, with its emphasis on export production and management by large commercial enterprises in a transnationalized economy, has become the worldwide program of the capitalist powers to re-create the world in their own image.

The impact of the economic growth model is not reserved for the Third World alone. It touches the First World too, not just by concentrating the world's wealth in fewer and fewer First World hands, but by progressively marginalizing poor and small producers who live among the rich. Progressive indebtedness and concentration of land among banks and corporations expel productive farmers from their lands even in the United States, and Amerindians face increasingly tough struggles with mining companies wanting the minerals under their soils. The economic growth model, so often hailed as the road to worldwide prosperity, hardly bodes well for the poor and their land.

CHAPTER 3

Land in the Biblical Tradition

The experience of Naboth and his vineyard is the Latin American experience. Listen to a peasant farmer from Brazil's impoverished northeast comment on 1 Kings 21:

Around here we don't have kings, but the big landowners have a vice: they like having more land . . . always more. It even seems they are made of greed.

King Ahab wanted a piece of Naboth's land for a garden. Pure greed! He must have had lots of land. What marks the will of the big owners is the abuse of power.

I think greed is more perfected now. Here in the northeast of Brazil they want land to plant sugar cane, to produce alcohol [for automotive fuel], or to plant grass for beef cattle and then export the meat. Nothing to produce food, something good, for the people!

And the people without land, without the power to plant, who are hungry? I myself haven't eaten meat since a year ago.

The way Ahab and his wife Jezebel got Naboth out of their path is the same today. They use lies and falsify documents to "prove" that they are the owners. Liars! They get false testimonies, they buy witnesses. Sometimes they

order the murder of small farmers. That's what the proph-
et Elijah says here: they are thieves and murderers.

I like Naboth's reply to the king: "The Lord forbid that
I should give you the inheritance of my fathers." Small
farmers honor their little pieces of land. It has a history.
Generally it is a history of sweat and suffering. To give up
land to the big owners is to erase that history that comes
from so long ago, from grandparents, from one's parents.[1]

For Latin American peasant farmers, the story of Naboth and
his vineyard is a powerful representation of their own reality.
They see themselves as Naboth and his experience as their own.
For them, Ahab and Jezebel are no different from contemporary
large landowners and agricultural enterprises. Latin American
peasants understand that land is inheritance, but that for the
powerful, it is only a commodity to be bought and sold for personal gain. The story of Naboth is their story.

His story is found in 1 Kings 21, and is a good place to begin
a study of the biblical tradition of land. It lifts out the principal
feature of that tradition — namely, that land is inheritance — but
also makes clear that biblical land is soil to be tilled, and as
such, is a central justice concern. The biblical tradition of land
as inherited soil that signifies God's presence, and therefore
hope and future, is what makes that tradition meaningful to
Latin American peasants. Seen from their context of marginalization and struggle, they discover in the Bible a historic dimension of the land. At the same time, the biblical history of struggle
for land becomes their struggle for land even today.

As biblical tradition, the importance of land cannot be over-
estimated. Marcelo de Barros of Brazil and José Luis Caravias
of Ecuador affirm, "the theme of land is fundamental in the
biblical tradition." They explain, "The land, besides being an
object of study, also is the angle, the prism, the theological place
to view faith and life."[2] Walter Brueggemann, in his rich study
of the biblical land tradition, suggests that "land might be a way
of organizing biblical theology" as "a prism for biblical faith."[3]
Others have traced the history of salvation in the same terms,[4]
and have shown the tremendous importance, especially socio-

logical and ideological, that land played in the formation of Israel.[5]

LAND IN THE HEBREW BIBLE

Land is especially important in the Hebrew Bible. As Gerhard von Rad explains, "In the whole of the Hexateuch there is probably no more important idea than that expressed in terms of the land promised and later granted by Yahweh, an idea found in all the sources, and indeed in every part of them."[6] It is land that is promised to the patriarchs, and it is in hopeful expectation of that land that they begin their pilgrimage of faith that shapes the whole history of Israel.

DEFINITION OF LAND

When the Hebrew Bible speaks about promised land, it is talking about the earth and its resources, not a spiritual home. Anticipating modern economists who understand land not only as soil, but also as minerals, water, forest resources, even the air, the Deuteronomist spoke of:

> A good land, a land of brooks of water, of fountains and springs, flowing forth in valleys and hills, a land of wheat and barley, of vines and fig trees and pomegranates, a land of olive trees and honey, a land in which you will eat bread without scarcity, in which you will lack nothing, a land whose stones are iron, and out of whose hills you can dig copper. [Deut. 8:7–9]

This material reality of land is evident in the Hebrew words used for land. "Land" in the Hebrew Bible is used both as "nation" and as "cultivable soil." In Hebrew, *'erets*, the most commonly used word for "land," means "earth" as opposed to sky, and as nation or geographical territory. However, it also means cultivable soil and inhabitable place. The other word is *'adamah*, specifically signifying soil for cultivation, especially rich humus, as top soil. It is the patrimony of families and communities, and is the place where one establishes a home.[7] What is important to note is that "land" always means cultivable and fertile soil where one establishes a home in order to sustain life. It is this sense that has meaning for Latin American peasants, and is the sense emphasized in this study.

Still, for peasants land is more than just dirt. It signifies a place, an identity, a history, and a future. Likewise in the Bible. Land always is simultaneously literal and symbolic. It signifies physical and existential well-being and security. As Brueggemann says, "[biblical] land is never simply physical dirt but is always physical dirt freighted with social meanings derived from historical experience."[8] This becomes clear as the Hebrew tradition unfolds.

LAND AS PROMISE AND GIFT

The essential affirmation of that tradition is that Yahweh promises land to the patriarchs as the foundation of the future, and that the promise is sealed in the exodus from Egyptian slavery. That promise has fundamental importance because it is the covenant that Yahweh makes to form and sustain the people of Israel. It is the beginning of their history. Land is given to them as a people and signifies their identity, the presence of Yahweh, and therefore, an open future (Exod. 6:6–8). This is summed up in the event of the exodus. Yahweh proves faithful to the covenant by freeing the Hebrews from Egypt so that they can enter the promised land (Exod. 3:7–8). Liberation and land became inseparably joined, and were seen as the ethical base for living in the land. Thus covenant—exodus—promised land form a single theological set or unit (Deut. 26:5–9).

These affirmations are seen clearly in Deuteronomy where land especially is significant. There, promise and gift are related integrally, and together signify past, present, and future. In other words, the promise given to the patriarchs in the past is actualized in the present, and corresponds to the salvific activity of Yahweh.[9] Von Rad comments, "The promise of land itself was proclaimed ever anew, even after its fulfillment, as a future benefit of God's redemptive activity."[10] Promised land is the moving force of history (Gen. 12:1–2), and is the frame of reference for the present and future. The promise always is before the people, and its possession is the gift of salvation.[11] With the promise, Israel knows that it has a future, in spite of being "the fewest of all peoples" (Deut. 7:7). The promise is gift; it is Yahweh who gives the land (Deut. 6:10–11). It is only necessary to possess it (Deut. 11:10–12).

HOW TO POSSESS THE LAND

Land is a gift. It is necessary only to take possession of it. However, this appears to be a contradiction because, at the same time that land is affirmed as a gift, Yahweh commands that the land be taken. Human action is required to possess the gift and to fulfill the promise. It is because Yahweh has given the land that it is possible to take it. The power of Yahweh assures the possession of the land (Deut. 3:21–22; 7:1–9, etc.), but people have to take it through their own struggle. This is the meaning of the constant refrain, "to take possession of the land which the Lord your God gives to you to possess." To take the land, then, is to fulfill Yahweh's command (Jos. 1:11).[12]

In need of land, they took it in various ways and proclaimed it as Yahweh's gift in fulfillment of his promises. They see all their military operations as guided by Yahweh who leads them out, sends fear upon the enemy, and gives Israel victory even against heavier odds. To take possession of the land is therefore for Israel an act of faith and obedience.[13]

This struggle for land is the foundation for the formation of Israel. Taking the land always has theological significance and always is justified as the promise of Yahweh. Taking the land is not to covet land. To covet it would be to seek one's own personal, selfish gain. Against that the scripture contains specific warnings (i.e., Deut. 10:11–20). Rather, it is to take in the sense of receiving what is necessary for life's well-being. Without land there is no life, and that Israel sharply felt.

It is not clear how, historically and sociologically, Israel took the land. Three major theories have been suggested: a slow process of immigration, a great military conquest, or a peasant rebellion.[14] Some recent studies contend that the most likely was a peasant rebellion.[15]

The background of the theory of the peasant rebellion is the tributary mode of production that formed the socio-historic context of Canaan. In this mode of production (sometimes called "Asiatic," following Karl Marx's usage) all land, farm animals, and crop seeds belonged to the king (or the state) who ruled over a given territory from a central city surrounded by villages and fields. Peasant farmers paid tribute to the king for the right to use his land, seed, and animals. In return, they received the king's protection. The king was aided by his military units, a bureaucracy geared to collecting the tribute and effecting public works and organizing agricultural production, and a religious apparatus to legitimize the system. Genesis 47:13–26 clearly illustrates this mode of production. (It also illustrates how adversity can benefit the powerful.) Jorge Pixley calls this mode of production the "sociological key" to reading the Bible because, he argues, "all the societies that enter in the biblical history of Israel can be understood as modifications of this system."[16]

At the time of the conquest, then, Canaan was characterized by the tributary mode of production with its system of city-states as power centers, supported by large agricultural estates worked by landless or near landless peasant farmers. These large estates were controlled by urban landlords who formed a socio-military elite that managed the state apparatus, maintaining their own dominion over the countryside. They themselves were under the jurisdiction of a king and all subject to the politico-military hegemony of Egypt.[17] Peasants were unable to control or enjoy the fruit of their own production. Their labor was appropriated by the powerful with little return for themselves:[18]

> Indebted peasants, deprived of independent means of subsistence, were recruited as cultivators of large estates and compelled to serve the onerous demands of overlords from whom they had little prospect of escape.[19]

Israelites, by then a people of agriculturists[20] as well as herders, looking for land, entered in the midst of this social context. In Canaan they found fertile land and social discontent. Indeed

Canaan was in decline as angry peasants and the ever-ready revolutionary brigands, *apiru*,[21] vented their frustration against the dominant system. The Canaanite peasants and *apiru* made common cause with the Israelites and together overthrew the feudallike system. In the process the Canaanite peasants and *apiru* were absorbed by Israel and converted to the religion of Yahweh. Indeed a compelling factor in their joining with Israel was that the religion of Yahweh offered a profound ideological base to support their cause. Whereas Baalism justified "Asiatic" society, Yahwism did not. The tradition of promised land as God's gift, and the divine command to take it, based on the celebration of a historical act of liberation from Egypt and an antifeudal, egalitarian commitment, easily attracted Canaan's disgruntled and oppressed rural population.

The history of peasants, both past and present, favors the "peasant rebellion" model. There is nothing new about land as the fundamental issue in peasant uprisings. It always has been the central issue. Likewise, utopic hopes and promises of a future re-created social order—such as the promised land tradition—"provide the ideological fuel," anthropologist Eric R. Wolf reminds us, "that drives the rebellious peasantry."[22] Furthermore, guerrilla insurgency is the mode of peasant warfare. The Hebrew Bible stories of Joshua easily are imagined by Latin American peasants as contemporary revolutionary movements. Indeed, Joshua far more fulfills the image of a charismatic guerrilla *commandant* than a military academy trained battalion commander. It also is difficult to conceive how a still unsettled people like the Hebrews could have obtained the arms, as well as the logistic and strategic know-how, in ways other than guerrilla hit-and-run tactics. There also is no reason to suppose that although peasants now are quite discontent, they were quite content back then. The history of many societies is replete with peasant rebellions. Right or wrong, it is the rebellion model that makes sense to Latin American peasants.

Following the conquest, Israel radically restructured living in the land, implementing a far-reaching land reform that changed the tributary social economic formation to one classically "peasant" (see chapter 2):

1. Land was placed under the authority of families, in the

first instance, with ultimate authority vested in the community. The community ultimately was responsible for the division and use of the land.

2. Production and consumption were oriented toward basic family needs, and only secondarily toward the market. This also assured that surplus production stayed in the community and was not siphoned off through tribute or other exploitive relationships.

3. Labor was provided by the family itself, and the community provided various types of mutual assistance.[23]

4. Existential identification was with the family plot and community in such a way that individual-family-community could not be separated. It was inheritance.

5. Basic social organizational structure was the village and community elders.

Purposefully there was no earthly king or centralized government. Pixley tells us:

> Characteristic of all the insurrectionary and migratory movements that formed the nation of Israel, was the rejection of kings (see Joshua 8:22–23; 9:7–15). And as monarchy was the only form of state that was known at that time, this signified a rejection of the state.[24]

As anthropologist Wolf explains:

> The peasant Utopia is the free village, untrammeled by tax collectors, labor recruiters, large landowners, officials. . . . Thus, for the peasant, the state is a negative quantity, an evil, to be replaced in short shrift by their own "homemade" social order.[25]

This basic socio-economic structure was legitimized by Yahwism, as we will see more clearly in the next section. But an important change was made regarding priests: unlike in the old tributary mode of production, priests were now excluded from the land. The Hebrews were aware of how, in the old order, the landed and politically privileged priesthood formed an ideological superstructure in the service of the king—that is, in the service of exploitation. Thus the new peasant Israelite society sought to avoid tempting Yahweh's priests with an economic base that would enable them to establish their own political power in the service of themselves—a temptation to which the church has often fallen.

What is abundantly evident in the "conquest" is that land as fertile, cultivable, and inhabitable soil, symbol of the fullness of salvation, promised to the landless, is an all surpassing factor in the formation of Israel.

LAND AS INHERITANCE AND SALVATION

The biblical presupposition is that the land belongs to Yahweh. "The earth is the Lord's," Psalm 24 affirms. "The land is mine," says Yahweh (Lev. 25:23). It is for this reason that Yahweh can give it. The idea that land belongs to Yahweh is a very old concept, possibly predating the tradition of the promise itself, and is of priestly origins.[26] This, of course, was of singular importance for the people of Israel. It meant, fundamentally, that they could not do with the land as they pleased. (Hence Naboth could not have sold his land to Ahab even if he had wanted to.) It was the principle behind legislation regulating the distribution and use of the land, as we shall see in a moment, and was intimately related to the concept of inheritance.

The verb "to inherit" or the phrase "as inheritance" is used frequently in relation to land, especially as "nation" but also in the sense of cultivable and inhabitable soil (Lev. 20:24; Num. 33:54; 34:2, 13, 16; 1 Kings 21:3; etc.).[27] Land is given as inheritance and although it is divided among the various tribes and then parceled among the many families, the concept of inheritance served to maintain the idea that Yahweh was the ultimate owner (over against a king or group of landlords). Von Rad explains that earth and soil "were granted to the clan by Yahweh as a fief which they were to cultivate."[28] Again, this reflects a peasant concept of landownership.

For the peasantry, land never is private in the capitalist sense of an autonomous right to use or dispose of it for private accumulation. Rather, each family receives perpetual right to use the land as a trust from the whole community. Ownership of the land must be understood in that communal context. This implies certain limitations—for example, that the family cannot transfer the land to nonpeasants, because the land cannot be alienated from its final owners, the community. As a Costa Rican peasant explained, "You can't sell land, because it's inheritance."

In the biblical tradition, inheritance unites the idea of Yahweh: giver of life—land: means of life, or Yahweh: giver of salvation—land: means of salvation. Theologically the one is identified with the other. This we see in the Psalms where the concept of "portion" is utilized:

> The Lord is my chosen portion and my cup;
> thou holdest my lot.
> The lines have fallen for me in pleasant places,
> Yea, I have a goodly heritage. [Ps. 16:5–6]

> I cry to thee, O Lord;
> I say, Thou art my refuge,
> my portion in the land of the living.
> [Ps. 142:5]

Here Yahweh is identified with "portion" and reference is made to casting lots. "Portion" is the plot of land that each family received as part of the "inheritance." As in all peasant societies, the "portion" was the center of family life and the basic unit of social organization. Lots were cast (cf. Num. 33:54; 34:13), which were believed to be divinely guided, to determine which plots were given to each family. These inalienable plots (Num. 36:6–9) were economically equal (again, a characteristic of peasants). Participation in the inheritance guaranteed a family the right to be included in the distribution of land, although not to a specific plot of their selection. What is interesting is that inheritance, concretized in the plot of cultivable and inhabitable soil, is identified with Yahweh-salvation. This is especially clear in Psalm 16:5–6. As Von Rad notes:

> The worshiper is so certain of being under the protection of Yahweh, the foundation of life, that he finds in the traditional Old Testament conception of the "portion" a

full and complete expression of all that his relationship with God guarantees to him.[29]

Inheritance signifies salvation, and that salvation is inseparable from the soil.

Contemporary expressions of land as inheritance can be observed in the ancient Andean concept of *pachamama* and the importance of the *milpa* in Central America.

For Andean Quechua and Aymara peoples, land is the presence of the *pachamama*, their mythico-religious concept of space. *Pacha* signifies the place of maximum security in the present, and is identified with the *ayllu* or the traditional Amerindian community with its fields for cultivation and pastures. *Mama*, as the feminine, maternalizes the *pacha* that manifests itself in the land. Thus, *pachamama* is understood as a maternal womb whose life-giving power materializes as cultivable and inhabitable soil.

In Central America, especially in Guatemala, the *milpa* or family corn field is the central axis of peasant life that organizes time and resources, and provides existential identification. Corn is the mythic substance of human genesis. Human beings are "people of corn." Wherever corn germinates, life germinates. Human beings live in a symbiotic relationship to the *milpa*.

Through *pachamama* and *milpa* we can begin to grasp the significance of inheritance for the ancient Hebrews:

> But the meek shall possess the land, and delight themselves in abundant prosperity. [Ps. 37:11]

> Blessed are the meek, for they shall inherit the earth. [Matt. 5:5]

Or, as they sing in Nicaragua, "Let's go to the *milpa*, the *milpa* of the Lord . . ."

Inheritance functions theologically to express that land is Yahweh's property and, at the same time, that the fullness of salvation implies a historical dimension. It is to live in the security of having fertile and cultivable soil to establish one's home. It is to have a *milpa*.

LIVING IN THE LAND

Promised land is the promise of life. As Von Rad demonstrates,[30] "life" was an essential theological concept for Israel: "choose life, that you and your descendants may live" (Deut. 30:19). Life is what land means. It is, above all, sustenance.

Throughout the Hebrew Bible land tradition, one finds a symbiotic relationship between human life and the soil. First, according to the scripture, humankind even is created of soil, *adamah*, hence the name Adam. Humanity is part of the soil itself.[31] Land then becomes a work project to sustain human life (Gen. 1:28–29; 2:15; and put negatively, Gen. 3:17–19). Humanity is to manage, care for, and use the land and its creatures to ensure a full and plentiful life, thus, secondly, making soil truly soil. Land and humankind depend upon each other for each other's fulfillment.

Nor is anyone to be excluded from the land. This is glimpsed in the Cain and Abel story, and seen more fully in the Abraham and Lot account. For the writers of the account of Cain and Abel, Cain as a sedentary farmer represented landowners, while Abel, the shepherd, represented the landless nomad. The sociohistorical situation of the writers was one of conflict between these two groups, a serious problem for early Israel (Num. 21:21–23). When the gift of the landless was received by God but that of the landed rejected, Cain rose up against Abel. Cain sought to exclude Abel from access to land and was punished by Yahweh for doing so.[32] Land is to be shared.

A similar situation is faced by Abraham and Lot (Gen. 13:1–18), where the two men were in conflict over access to pasture (land). Instead of fighting, however, Abraham offers to share his land with Lot, giving him the territory of Lot's choosing. The problem is solved by finding ways to include each other, not exclude each other, from the land. By sharing land Abraham becomes a source of life for Lot and permits Yahweh's blessing to come upon both of them. Abraham "gives" land to Lot, just as Yahweh "gives" land to Abraham (and Israel).[33] Exclusion means murder, death, while inclusion means blessing, life. Land is to be shared.

However, if this is true, what about the Conquest? Latin

American peasants will always ask why it was just to expel
Canaanite peasants from their land so Israel could take it. A
good question! The "peasant rebellion" model of the Conquest
provides an answer: Canaanite peasants in fact did not lose land,
rather, they received land—they were included in the inheritance—as they joined with Israel to overthrow the kings and the
landlords.

Because shared access to land was so central, it was very
important to regulate living in the land. Inclusion had to be
assured. This was a priestly function because it concerned life
itself, but had to be expressed in terms of socio-political organization. As Gottwald observes:

> The Israelite society was characterized by profound resis-
> tance and opposition to the forms of political domination
> and social stratification that had become normative in the
> chief cultural and political centers of the ancient Near
> East.[34]

Therefore, living in the land had to be governed in order "to
escape imperialism and feudalism imposed by outside powers
and to prevent the rise of feudal domination within their own
society."[35]

We find a concrete expression of this concern in the Levitical
laws about land management. Land could not be sold in perpetuity; the original owner had the right to repurchase the land;
nor could land be lost because of indebtedness (Lev. 25:23–28).
Speculation in the sale of land was prohibited (Lev. 25:14–17).
At the same time the concentration of land was prohibited and
property lines inviolable (Deut. 19:14). The poorest and those
without legal rights because they were foreigners, or those who
had no families to care for them and to give them a share in the
family inheritance, always were to have access to the fruit of the
land (Lev. 23:22). At bottom, agricultural production was to
have a social function. Just as no one could be excluded from
the land, likewise no one could be excluded from the fruit of
the land. It was prohibited to deceive the poor or to take advantage of their economic condition for personal gain (Lev. 25:35–
38). The poor, who for economic circumstances had to offer

themselves as day laborers, were to receive a just salary. Slavery or forced labor was prohibited (Lev. 25:39–40), at least in perpetuity. Every sabbatical and jubilee year the land was to "rest" and liberty and restoration as an act of social leveling were to be proclaimed (Lev. 25; Deut. 15, note especially 15:4).

The sabbatical was every seventh year; slaves and day laborers were to be freed (Ex. 21:2), debts canceled (Deut. 15:12), and the land to lie fallow, that is "to rest" (Lev. 25.1–7). These obviously were important provisions to ensure socio-economic equality, or at least to diminish the exploitive domination of one group over another. The third provision, that of allowing the land to rest, meant two things, both integrally related to the first two provisions: giving to the poor and landless free use of the land for their well-being as they sought to re-establish themselves upon their newly regained freedom (Ex. 23:10–11); and leaving the land fallow (Lev. 25:4). Leaving the land fallow was of critical ecological importance for maintaining fertility and controlling plant diseases. Proper ecological management entered into the scheme of human justice because it was necessary to ensure that the land continually produced for human need. Not to respect the ecology of the land would be an injustice to human life, particularly the poorest. As a peasant farmer from Brazil reflects on this passage:

> Those laws are a little complicated . . . will they work like that? One thing is certain and I have experience of that: tired land dies little by little until it can't give more. Land has strength but it needs caring treatment.
>
> Imagine if today the big landowners let their land rest every seven years! Here in the northeast of Brazil, what they are doing is killing the land! And they aren't going to let it rest. You have to make it produce, without stopping.
>
> I'd like to see that thing of Jubilee! Land returned to its old owners.
>
> The owner of the land ought to be the one who takes from it things for life. When justice works right, it's the good law for all, for the countryside too.

Although how and where the institution of sabbath rest came about is uncertain, the practice emerged from God's resting on the seventh day of creation (Gen. 2:1–3). God's rest was understood as a sign of Yahweh's covenant with creation, affirming not only that it was good, but that God's presence continued. Human rest was seen as a gift from Yahweh for their well-being, for their protection, and for living in peace (Deut. 12:9–10; 25:19; Jos. 1:13; 11:23; 21:43–45).[36] Theologically, its practice signaled faith and trust in the creator God who was confident enough in the future to rest, yet still pass on creation as a gift to humanity. It meant that ultimately the world was in God's hands. Because it meant the establishment of peace and the end of exploitation and domination, as well as respect for the created order, it also symbolized the kind of world Yahweh willed. Thus sabbath rest was itself a promise for humanity.[37]

Whereas the sabbath year attempted to assure the relative restructuring of society at frequent intervals, the jubilee year (Lev. 25:8–34) meant land reform as the basis for radical socioeconomic restructuring every fiftieth year.[38] The jubilee was an intensification of the sabbath year, basically requiring the same provisions: 1) leaving the land fallow; 2) canceling debts; 3) freeing slaves, debtors, and servants; and 4) returning lands to original family owners.[39] That year all the Levitical laws were to be enforced and everyone, rich and poor, was to be placed on the same level. Only in that way could justice for the poorest be assured. Jubilee was the prophetic vision of a truly just and egalitarian society. Such utopic envisioning is not uncommon in peasant societies. What is significant about the jubilee legislation is that it represents an effort to give historic expression to their vision of a just society.

Behind the Levitical legislation, as we have seen, is the idea that Yahweh is the owner of the land. The land is Yahweh's, not an individual person's. In reality, the Israelites did not conceive of a system of private property. Instead of individuals, legal property was granted to the tribe, as Yahweh's representative.[40] It was the tribe, the community, that was responsible for dividing and managing land in Yahweh's name. Families and individuals enjoyed the land in usufruct. At bottom, land was given to the community as social property.

As the years passed, Israel found itself struggling to maintain the integrity of land and to avoid essentially tributary or feudallike relations. Israel faced growing land concentration in great estates, land speculation, forced labor, and exploitation of rural workers, the taking of lands in payment for debts, excessive taxes levied against peasant farmers, and deception and illegal means, even violence, in obtaining lands that increasingly were concentrated in the hands of a wealthy, royal elite. When the people begged for a king, Yahweh responded through Samuel, warning:

> He will take the best of your fields and vineyards and olive orchards. ... He will take the tenth of your grain and of your vineyards ... and the best of your cattle and your asses. [1 Sam. 8:14–16]

Yahweh's warning proved true. At his coronation, Saul owned only small property (1 Sam. 9:1b; 11:5) but shortly thereafter was able to give his officials estates (1 Sam. 22:7). He died leaving sizable land holdings (2 Sam. 9:9–10).[41] Solomon, urban and rich, drafted peasants for forced public works (1 Kings 5:13). Later Omri changed "Yahweh's gift" into a consumer article, dealing in land (1 Kings 16:24), thus instituting a concept of land alien to inheritance and the history of the promise. Ahab, with his wife Jezebel, followed the policies of his father Omri. When Naboth refused to sell his land, he was murdered and Ahab took the land (1 Kings 21). These events we can assume were not isolated, but representative of common practices among royalty and the upper class, institutionalized over the years.

Increasingly the rural population became the victim of violence and exploitation. With Amos and later Isaiah and Micah, and then Jeremiah and Ezekiel, we can see that happening. At the same time, the prophets underline the supreme importance that just land management had for Yahwism.

Amos's harsh words against those who exploited the poor are well known:

> The social context framing his words was an antisocial struggle by the owners of large landed estates, the stewards of the royal domain, to expand the size of their property.

This struggle for expansion helps explain the systematic way in which the rich proceeded against the small farmers: exacting of exorbitant taxes (5:11), the blocking of lawsuits and claims for compensation by bribing judges and legal maneuvering and finally buying up of their victims as slaves for a paltry sum. [8:6; see 2:6][42]

Both Isaiah (5:8) and Micah (2:15) condemned the upper class because it consolidated landholdings by taking land from peasant farmers. Land no longer signified "life," but avarice, commerce, and power.

The prophets constantly condemned the influence of Baalism, the Caananite religion. For them injustice as it related to tenancy and use of the land had its origin in the religion of Baal. Baalism also was a religion of the land. That was the reason for the fertility motif and cultic prostitution. But it represented a concept of land fundamentally different from that of the religion of Yahweh. For Baalism, land was a consumer item, not an "inheritance." Baal was the god of landlords, not peasants. To condemn Baalism, then, also was to condemn institutionalized injustices encrusted in land management. The prophets clearly saw the danger of losing all that had been gained in the "peasant rebellion" that gave birth to peasant Israel.

Indeed, this was the principal reason for the exile. The ancient concept of land had been abandoned and the sabbath rest "profaned" because its provisions assuring justice for the poorest had become no more than empty words (Jer. 34; Ezek. 22). Turning the land into a consumer item to bring power and wealth led to Yahweh's punishment by taking the land away.

The original peasant mode of production of newly liberated Israel had given way to a nation-state dominated by a military and political elite. For the prophets, "peasant" remained the norm, their frame of reference for denouncing the injustices of kingly Israel. The future required a return to the past. Indeed, Ezekiel's visionary land reform of a restored Israel (Ezek. 37) projected the recovery of that peasant past as the beginning of a renewed Israel.[43]

Out of the Hebrew Bible tradition, at least six fundamental themes regarding land emerge: 1) land is a gift from Yahweh to sustain human life, both physically and existentially; 2) human action is required to secure the gift of land, but land must not be avariciously coveted; 3) land belongs to Yahweh but is trusted to the community in representation of Yahweh; 4) land is to be shared so that all might have access to life; 5) land is to be justly managed, and the measure of justice is the degree to which the poorest enjoy the benefits of the land; and 6) land itself must be respected so that it will produce for human need.

In the Hebrew Bible, then, land is socio-theological. It pertains to the essence of present and future human life. Land is promise and salvation; identity and presence of Yahweh. It is sustenance and power, security because it is inheritance.

LAND IN THE NEW TESTAMENT

The theme of "land" as a definable socio-theological concern is more difficult to trace in the New Testament. Nevertheless, land is not forgotten and the theme is reworked in various forms, with perhaps its clearest expression given by Jesus. The evangelists presuppose the tradition of the land. Paul utilizes important land themes. For the writers of Hebrews and Revelation, land is the great eschatological symbol.

Nevertheless, few recognize land in the New Testament as a concern for rural justice, as cultivable soil and a place to live. Land in the New Testament appears to be so spiritualized as to lose practically all earthly quality. Land is eschatological, a promise fulfilled in Jesus. It "is struggle, thesis, antithesis, and we journey even today, toward synthesis in Christ."[44] Land in the New Testament is "land that has been resurrected in Christ."[45] "Place for habitation" no longer is on earth, but in heaven. Land is completely deterritorialized.[46] The promised land loses its historical anchorage in order to be subsumed by the great spiritual promise of the future. Thus W. D. Davies, in his massive study of the land as Jewish territorial doctrine, concludes that rejection, spiritualization, historical concern, and sacramental concentration have been the principal attitudes toward the land that have informed the history of Christianity. In essence, he argues, the person of Jesus Christ takes the place of land.[47]

LAND IN THE EPISTLES

In Paul (and Pauline writings) it would appear that this is true. Although land themes are prominent, they are treated quite differently than in the Hebrew Bible. In Romans, Abraham is the paradigm of faith. However, for Paul, the promise Abraham received through faith is no longer land, but salvation, expressed in terms of a profound spiritual relationship. Likewise inheritance, as in Ephesians, no longer is a plot of cultivable soil as well as a divine-human relationship, but is a "general term which expresses the totality of future blessings to which the obedient Christian may look forward when the 'Kingdom of Christ and God' (Eph. 5:5) is fully present."[48]

The themes continue to provide rich imagery and carry profound concepts from the Hebrew Bible tradition of land, but they clearly have been reworked to carry other significance. However, it is important to recognize that Paul's concern is to show that the promise continues.[49] As Brueggemann writes, "The assertions of Paul are about living faithfully in history, about being secure in a world which promises no security, about having a place in a displacing world."[50] Certainly other Pauline themes, not related to land, offer fruitful possibilities for ministry concerned with contemporary land justice. Unity and solidarity, reconciliation with justice, love, all are important theological themes that undergird movements for justice in the land. Although the land theme has been reworked, land in the Hebrew Bible tradition is not neglected but enriched by the new Pauline insights.

The same is true in Hebrews where "rest," an important land theme, is given a central theological role, but also reelaborated to be relevant to other theological concerns. Hebrews 3–4 tell us that God's promise for God's people is not land but "rest," "a sabbath rest" (4:9) for the faithful. Apparently it no longer is related to land management. But here also rest is dynamic in character. It becomes prophetic, looking backward not only to God's rest on the seventh day, but thrusting forward "to a yet unfinished work of God."[51] Through present faith, one can enjoy rest even while looking forward to it in the future.

As we have seen, rest is about living in the land. It means

peace and righteousness (Heb. 12:14). Thus, as one interpreter observes:

> We might translate "rest" as resolution of turmoil (peace) and rectifying wrong (righteousness or justice). In personal terms this meant fulfillment in doing what was right, not inaction assumed in pious poses. In social terms, this meant justice pervading harmony in all God's creation, not order with unredressed exploitation.[52]

This, of course, means that the rest in Hebrews is exceedingly rich for a theology of land concerned with justice for the poor of the land. Also, we can see that Hebrews has not interpreted away the original meaning of rest, for rest in the Hebrew Bible always has a spiritual dimension as a dialectic within historical land management. It is, fundamentally, about living in the land in peace and righteousness.

Before turning to the Gospels, it will be instructive to examine briefly the Letter of James. By lifting up the plight of rural agricultural workers, James emphasizes landlessness as a specific justice concern. James condemns (the only specific sin he condemns) the rich landowners for defrauding day laborers of their wages (5:4). The concentration of land in great estates meant a mass of landless rural laborers easily exploitable because of their dependent condition. Then as now the landowners simply withheld their wages, in effect, robbing them. James condemns the practice as fraud.[53] The wages of day laborers were very small and not paying them the little they earned was a serious offense.[54] Thus the defrauded laborers justifiably "cry out" to "the Lord of hosts" (5:4). This is an allusion to the Hebrew Bible tradition that withholding wages of the poor was a particularly serious offense meriting the poor's "cry . . . to the Lord" (Deut. 24:14–15; see also Jer. 22:13; Mal. 3:5) seeking retribution.[55]

Latin American peasants understand what James is getting at. Again from Brazil:

> That James is a person who knew close up the oppression of small farmers and the misery of the big estates!

He talks about those who steal our salaries. Here, in this region, all the property owners enrich themselves at the cost of rural workers. They even prohibit us from cutting and selling the coconuts from the coconut groves on the land we rent!

And it's sure certain that they get fat and live in shining luxury at the expense of our ribs! My boss lives in Recife, a big city, in a little palace. His kids study in other countries. He has four cars in the garage!

My family hasn't eaten meat in a year. In the past, you ate what you planted. Now we only have grass for cattle (for export), and sugar cane for alcohol. When will that change?

Saint James says their gold is going to rust and moths will eat their clothes. But it's taking too long!

One screams. The Bible says that God hears the cry of the poor. But I think the cry of the small farmers has to go up together with our struggle step by step.

One day there has to be agrarian reform, reform of everything, prepared by the poor. That will be the day our cry is answered.

As James recognized, New Testament land is not only spiritual but also temporal. Brueggemann notes that in the New Testament, "the promissory language is focused on land and surely cannot be understood apart from it. And no matter how much it has been spiritualized, it is probable that the image is never robbed of its original, historical referent."[56] This we can see in the Synoptic Gospel tradition.

THE GOSPELS AND THE LAND

The evangelists are quite clear that Jesus came preaching the reign of God. That reign not only is spiritual, but has an equally important historical dimension. Future spiritual reality is related dialectically to present historical reality, the two held together in constant tension as a continuum. The reign even requires the radical inversion of historical reality—the blind see, the lame walk, the first are the last and the last are the first, outcasts are invited to the sovereign's banquet, and the Good News is preached to the poor. The very heart of Jesus' preaching is this historical rupture and radical realignment of the socio-historical relationship as both anticipation and presence of the reign of God. The concept of *koinonia* is the historical organizing principle of the reign. Jesus' followers in the early church sought to create communities characterized by solidarity and profound sharing of their lives, including their material goods. They lived the eschatological reign as a present reality.

The socio-theological background of the reign is the Hebrew Bible concept of jubilee. As discussed earlier in this chapter, jubilee was about justice in the land, about assuring the poor access to the land for their well-being. Fundamentally it was about social leveling to avoid domination, and therefore exploitation, by more powerful social-economic groups over weaker ones. When Jesus announced the reign of God it was impossible for his hearers not to have thought of jubilee.

It is even possible that Jesus consciously was proclaiming a new jubilee. His selection of Isaiah 61:1–2, a jubilee passage, as his inaugural sermon (Luke 4:16–21) would suggest that. Several scholars believe he did and they have shown the intimate relationship between Jesus' reign preaching and jubilee teaching.[57]

With this background, two of Jesus' teachings, that about debts and about land, both from the Sermon on the Mount, have considerable importance.

In the so-called Beatitudes, Jesus preaches, "Blessed are the meek, for they shall inherit the earth" (Matt. 5:5). These words of Jesus are those of Psalm 37:11, where, as we have seen, one finds the concept of "land-inheritance-salvation." It is possible that the social context of the psalm was one of conflict over land, and Jesus picks up the same theme and preaches it in his own context of landlessness. As presented by Matthew, "the earth" (the land) appears to be an eschatological earth and the "meek" spiritualized. The original context of Jesus, however, offers another interpretation.

The Sermon on the Mount forms part of the logia of Jesus. As a "sermon" it represents a collection of Jesus' original sayings as remembered by the primitive church. The original context and significance of those sayings were quite different from Matthew's, or at least from Matthew's concerns.

In Jesus' time, landlessness and the exploitation of rural laborers were among the most serious injustices suffered by Palestinian peasants. Foreign absentee landlords increasingly concentrated land in their own hands and dominated the whole geographic area, especially Galilee. As Joachim Jeremias tells us:

It is necessary to realize that not only the whole of the upper Jordan valley, and probably the north and the north-west shores of the Lake of Gennesaret as well, but also a large part of the Galilean uplands, were parceled out as latifundio, and that these Galilean latifundios were, for the most part in the hands of foreign landlords.[58]

As a result, virtually all larger local landholders had lost their independence and the small farmers had lost their land. Commercial agriculture and agribusiness related to processing agricultural products were increasingly lucrative because of the demands of the city of Jerusalem and the commercial interests of Rome,[59] thus sharpening social conflict by creating a great mass of rural day laborers dominated by a small landowning elite. This situation is reflected in several of Jesus' parables (Matt. 18:21–35; 2:1–16; 21:33–45).

From the years that preceded Jesus' birth until the destruction of the temple, the Palestinian peasantry was a constant source of social and political instability as it struggled against the dominant social sectors and the Roman invaders. These popular rural movements assumed the social forms of banditry and messianic personages, as well as organized subversive movements that practiced a kind of guerrilla warfare seeking to reclaim the rights of the poor. At the same time there occurred a resurgence of prophecy also from within the peasantry. The new prophets, as exemplified by John the Baptist, scorched not only the Romans, but also the dominant social and religious sectors whom, they believed, collaborated with Rome and oppressed the rural masses.[60]

In this context, Jesus preached that the "meek" would receive land. The meek, coming from Psalm 37:11, are the poor, the *anawim.*[61] The *anawim* were the afflicted, the pushed-down, the indigent, the tormented, the exploited and oppressed. They were also humble, open, and faithful,[62] in contrast to the prideful and disloyal.[63] The meek are poor, marginalized people, not the passive, patient, and long-suffering, divorced from social reality and identified only in a spiritual plane. Given the socio-historical context of Jesus, the "meek" had to have been landless peasants forcibly converted to day laborers or minifundistas by the owners of great estates.

Certainly Jesus had a public ready to listen. His preaching about land for the landless was directed to a real situation that determined life and death for the rural majorities.

Thus the Hebrew Bible concept of land-inheritance-salvation had a central place in Jesus' reign-jubilee preaching. While land in his preaching also is eschatological, it is eschatological with a historical dimension directly related to cultivable and fertile soil as a salvation promise to landless peasant farmers. Land was a central theme of Jesus' message.

Jesus also taught his disciples to pray, "And forgive us our debts, as we also have forgiven our debtors" (Matt. 6:12). Cancelation or "forgiveness" of debts was an important jubilee theme, here represented by Jesus also in his Sermon on the Mount and one very dear to Palestinian peasants.

Again, the socio-historical context is important if we are to understand the significance of Jesus' words for landless peasant farmers. Because of progressive indebtedness, the formally free peasant landowners "had been reduced to the practical equivalent of slavery."[64] Heavy taxation policies by Herod the Great forced smallholders to borrow heavily, putting up their land as security. Unable to pay their debts, they lost their land, often becoming laborers and sharecroppers for the new owners. Still, as John Howard Yoder explains:

> The problem of the peasant was not thereby resolved. His unpaid debts continued to pile up to astronomical levels. Then, in order to regain his funds, the creditor ordered that the sharecropper should be sold with his wife and children and all his possessions in order to cover the debts.[65]

Thus debt was one of the institutionalized means whereby land was concentrated in the hands of the wealthy, capital transferred to the rich, and a large supply of cheap or free agricultural labor assured. Although only fragments remain (Matt. 6:12, cf. Matt. 18:21–35), teaching about debt must have been another central theme of Jesus' reign teaching that was directly related to the injustice of landlessness.

LAND–PLACE FOR THE NEW

"Promised land" in the biblical tradition is "the gift of a radically different situation," as Gustavo Gutiérrez says. Isaiah's promise of "new heavens and a new earth" (Is. 65:27) finally is the promise of "a new situation wherein joy will take root in the fulfilled promise that justice would be established."[66]

Wolf points out:

> The peasant experience tends to be dualistic, in that he is caught between his understanding of how the world ought to be properly ordered and the realities of a mundane existence, beset by disorder. Against this disorder, the peasant has always set his dreams of deliverance. ... The true order is yet to come.[67]

Such utopic visions as found in Isaiah, Ezekiel, and Micah show how keenly such visions of the future drove Israel in its dreams for a just society.

It is this same utopic dream of a new earth that is taken up by the writer of Revelation. Land again has central prominence, now as the great eschatological symbol of hope and justice. There is to be "a new heaven and a new earth," where God, now dwelling with the people, "will wipe away every tear from their eyes, and death shall be no more, neither shall there be mourning nor crying nor pain anymore, for the former things have passed away" (Rev. 21:1, 3, 4–5). Land is not just dirt, nor is it simply to be distributed. Rather, land is the place for something new to happen, where justice, hope, and well-being become part of history.

We can see, then, that the land tradition is very much part

of the New Testament and that even with its reworking retains the same justice concerns that the Hebrew Bible has for the poor of the land. These New Testament concerns not only condemn exploitation and require doing justice, but especially exalt the poor in the eyes of God.

CONCLUSION

The theological framework for a "theology of the land" that emerges from the Hebrew and New Testament biblical traditions are the twin units of 1) covenant—exodus—promised land and 2) jubilee—reign of God. The exodus tradition of liberation from slavery finds its fulfillment in the promised land. The jubilee traditions seek to incarnate in history the creation and maintenance of a social order based on justice and egalitarianism. The reign of God unites these historic traditions with the preaching of Jesus and the concerns of the apostolic church.

Together these traditions show that the purpose of the land is to provide for life: life that means justice and well-being, existential security, and history reordered for the poor. They suggest that land, cultivable soil, is due the dispossessed not only for their well-being but also as the anticipation of salvation itself. They want to show that God's promise continues, not just as a spiritual future, but as a historical reality of peace and righteousness. They are concerns for the radical inversion of history that will make that promise a reality, as *koinonia* manifested in all human relationships. In an important sense, land is displaced by Jesus Christ, not in the sense of negating, but rather fulfilling. Indeed, it was he who announced the Good News of God's reign to the poor of the land.

CHAPTER 4

The Church and the Challenge of Land

During the 1980s, land emerged as a central pastoral and theological concern for the Latin American church. As never before, church leaders spoke out against the injustices suffered by the poor of the land. Priests and pastors made the cause of the rural poor their own. Pastoral letters on the problem of land were published by Catholic bishops in Brazil (1980), Paraguay (1983), Chile (1984), Peru (1986), Ecuador (1986), Guatemala (1988), and Panama (1988). Among Protestants, the Council of Latin American Churches (CLAI) made land and indigenous peoples a program concern. The Latin American network related to the Commission of the Churches' Participation in Development of the World Council of Churches launched cooperative programs on the question of land.

By the end of the decade, pastoral workers involved in the issue of land and the poor were organizing into networks across the region to share their ministries with each other, analyze together their situations, and offer mutual support. A new ministerial form—ministry from the land—*pastoral de la tierra*—took its place alongside other long-standing ministries.

THE CHURCH AS LANDLORD IN THE HISTORY OF LATIN AMERICA

The Latin American church has not always been so concerned with land as a central justice issue. Indeed, Spanish conquistadores, *hacendados*, agri-businessmen, and transnationals have not been the only landlords in Latin America. The church has been a landlord too. During the colonial and republican periods, the church acquired vast tracts of land, not only for evangelistic and educational purposes, but especially for commercial interests.

The church was not supposed to own land in colonial America. It was illegal, but laws were easily circumvented. Also the clergy differed over the propriety of being landlords. Nevertheless, by the end of the sixteenth century in Mexico, for example, the church had become one of the New World's great landowners. This was accomplished either by direct ownership of estates, or through wills and legacies granting the church perpetual income from others' land. The phenomenon was evident throughout colonial America, and became a source of concern to the Spanish Crown:

In 1608–1609 the viceroy of Peru, the viceroy of Mexico, and all the Audiencias in the Americas were ordered to furnish information about the rapid cornering of land "by the religious," which, it was declared, owned a third of the estates.[1]

In spite of the liberal reforms following independence, the church continued to amass land well into the twentieth century. By 1905, for instance, the church was the largest landowner in Ecuador, and in Bolivia it owned many large estates until the 1953 land reform. These church estates were no different from any other. Like all haciendas, they relied on feudal-type labor relations to turn a profit. Like the other landlords, the church's interests were those of the landed aristocracy.

It was not until the middle of the nineteenth century and the first part of the twentieth that Protestant missions were successfully established in Latin America. Their principal interest was the saving of souls and wresting Latin America from the Roman Catholics. They hardly were important landholders, but land nevertheless did offer opportunities, both evangelistic and financial, for their missions (and in some cases, personal). Many missions hoped to establish profit-making farms to support their work and train peasants in modern agricultural techniques. Few of those efforts proved successful. At the same time, their mission stations often have been entry platforms for opening Amerindian lands to mining and lumber companies, cattlemen, and others, and with them, deadly diseases. Perhaps unconsciously, but Protestant "pacification and civilizing" of forest Amerindians has served well the interests of dominant economic groups intent on taking land.

In some cases, however, Protestant missions tried to turn land into models of rural justice. In the 1940s and 50s, in Ecuador and Bolivia, Protestants effected land reforms by turning their haciendas over to the peasants who worked them. Perhaps the most significant effort was by Canadian Baptists on their Huatajata Hacienda on the shores of Lake Titicaca in Bolivia. From its beginning in 1911, the estate had been run by missionaries like most other haciendas. Finally in the 1930s, a Baptist observer reported that "it finally dawned upon the unselfish staff that their position as landholders was speaking more loudly than their words of salvation."[2] In 1942, serfdom was abolished and the major part of the land distributed among the Amerindians. This experiment later served as a model for the far-reaching Bolivian land reform in 1953.

In spite of such efforts, however, the story of Protestant rural missions has been largely one of owning and operating mission farms. They may have affected farming practices in some small measure, but they certainly did not confront the matter of land control and landlessness in any significant way.

THE CHURCH'S NEW RESPONSE TO LAND

If historically the church has sided with the powerful landlords, there are important signs that the church is changing. Increasingly its identity is with the poor of the land, not the comfortable landowners as in the past. Land is no longer understood as real estate to be acquired for power and wealth. Rather, important sectors of the Roman Catholic Church, and occasionally Protestants, more and more are involved in the struggle for land reform and rural justice.

In Honduras priests have been actively involved in organizing unions of landless farmers to struggle for land. The vicariat of Yoró has assumed *pastoral de la tierra* as its mission priority. Facing international mining interests, Protestants and Catholics in Panama joined together to defend Guaymi Indian rights to their traditional territories. Church workers in Peru and Bolivia long have been active in the struggle for rural justice. The Venezuelan Catholic hierarchy has declared its support for the "defense of indigenous peoples and their legitimate right to the land they need for their social, cultural, and economic organization." The Venezuelan Pentecostal Evangelical Union has emphasized land as a central pastoral concern. In Paraguay Roman Catholics, Mennonites, and Disciples of Christ have bought land for indigenous communities, to assure their rights. In Chile and Ecuador, bishops have taken church lands and turned them over to the poor. Throughout the Latin American church, "land" is emerging as a central justice issue intimately related to the rights of rural peoples.

This same theme has been urged by the World Council of Churches (WCC). In a special declaration on "Land Rights for Indigenous People," the Central Committee called on member churches to:

> 1. listen to and learn from indigenous people in order to deepen Christian understanding of (and solidarity with) their legal rights, their political situation, their cultural achievements and aspirations, and their spiritual convictions;
> 2. commit significant financial and human resources to the struggle of indigenous people for land rights;
> 3. become politically involved on the side of indigenous peoples and join the struggle against those powers and principalities that seek to deny the land rights and human rights of indigenous people;
> 4. support indigenous people struggling for land rights

in their efforts to build linkage with other indigenous people around the world;

5. as a sign to the wider community of the churches' commitment to justice for indigenous people:

    a. to recognize the rightful claims of indigenous people and take steps to transfer land and property to them;

    b. to set up procedures to deal with the claims or demands of the indigenous people made upon the churches;

    c. to support the struggle of the people in their land claims through national and international courts of law;

6. examine their investments in national and transnational corporations with a view to taking action to combat corporate policies affecting the lands of indigenous people;

7. urge their governments to ratify and implement all relevant United Nations and other intergovernmental instruments for the protection of the rights of indigenous people;

8. urge their governments to enact adequate and effective national legislation recognizing the collective property of indigenous people.[3]

The Council of Latin American Churches, following the WCC example, has reminded its members:

The church must be alert to denounce the invasion of indigenous peoples' lands, to defend them in situations that require firm action by Christians in order to preserve them from the humiliation to which they are subjected in our continent, and take concrete measures in order to prevent their complete extermination. . . . *The struggle of indigenous peoples for their right to land is challenging the Church to be faithful to the Gospel of reconciliation and the biblical affirmation that all human beings are created in the image of God.*[4]

PASTORAL LETTERS ON LAND

The pastoral letters on land that Latin America's Roman Catholic bishops issued during the 1980s responded directly to their national situations, and are products of actual pastoral experience amid the reality of conflict. The letters are prophetic, seeking to provoke national discussion on the urgency of land in the national political economy, and commit the church and its pastors to ministries of rural justice and the defense of the poor of the land.

The letters begin with discussions of the urgency of the problem of land from the perspective of indigenous and peasant peoples. The bishops of Ecuador from the Amazonian region see "the clear primacy of the land above any other urgent problem." Land "concerns a dramatic problem whose roots we must seek not only in the current model of socio-economic development, but also in the conception and application of a determined policy of distribution and exploitation of land," the Paraguayan bishops write. "The principal struggle continues to be the struggle for land," the Peruvian bishops explain.

Continuing this same concern, the bishop of the vicariat of Darién in Panama raises a series of hard questions:

a. If the land is for all, why do some have none or very little and of poor quality, while others have great expanses of prime quality?

b. If land is to produce bread, why is not necessary food produced, and why does malnutrition persist?

c. If rural workers should live off the fruits of their labor on the land, why do our products not have a market and receive a good price?

d. If we ought to feed and care for the land, why are the poor denied access to technology and financing?

e. If the land is for the one who works it, why are not titles given for individual or community property?

f. If the land is to cultivate, why do so many flee agricultural work, preferring salaries in the cities?

g. If the land is for peace and should be defended, why are there conflicts and little organization?

h. If the ecology was conserved for centuries, why today is it being destroyed?

i. If the actual structure does not favor the poor of the land, why is there not a true agrarian reform?

j. If those who first possessed this land were indigenous peoples, why today are they marginalized from it? The most serious rural problem at the national level is avarice and monopolization of land.

Each letter is the story of marginalization and expulsion of the poor from their lands and the consequent concentration of those lands in the hands of wealthy individuals and corporations. The bishops see land as the key factor for a more just political economy. As the Peruvian bishops continue, "the urgent solution of the problem of land is previous and necessary to the creation of a climate of peace and brotherhood, without which there can be no development," in their southern Andean region.

Another characteristic of the pastoral letters is the affirmation of indigenous culture, so intimately related to the land. They lift up a spirituality of the land as giver of life, as the "mother earth," as a source for a renewed vision of land justice that emphasizes the social value, as opposed to the private value, of land:

Andean history teaches us that land is the source of life. Peasants say, *"the pachamama gives us life as a mother, with her products, in order to share one with the other."* Besides an economic factor, the land above all is, for peasants, *"the place of communal fraternity."*

In Panama:

Kuna and Emberá History and Tradition speak of land and humanity as the work of Paba (Father God for the Kunas) and of Ankoré (the Good God for the Emberá). Between humanity and the earth, God wants harmony: social harmony filled with beauty, peace, and brotherhood. ... Paba/Ankoré made the earth ... all the fruits of Mother Earth must be shared with her children.

Several letters express concern for ecology. They relate the destruction of the natural environment to modern development and capitalist enterprise, and see it intimately related to justice for peasants and indigenous peoples. The Ecuadoran bishops refer to the "extreme fragility of the forest," so important to human life that "it ought to be considered as the patrimony of humanity." "The equilibrium between the person and nature in our missionary zone," the Panamanian bishop writes, "is threatened, has been broken, or is at the point of being broken. And with that, community and cultural traditions of food and production, of work and the felt presence of the Creator."

All the letters contain a biblico-theological reflection that accents especially the concept of God as creator and owner of the earth, who puts the land at the disposition of all humankind, but particularly the poor, for their well-being. Jesus' relationship with the poor and his preaching the reign of God is a continuation of that concern. "Jesus is born and lives in midst of the poor and centers his mission on announcing the liberating promise . . . the arrival of the reign," the Peruvian letter affirms. The letter from Panama reads:

> The mission of Jesus has its roots in "the people of the land," but also in the major history and tradition of his people, the tradition of the prophets, that "today is fulfilled" in him . . . it is the God of the poor, the God of the oppressed, the God of life, who proclaims a new year of Jubilee for the landless that resounds in the words of Jesus.

Finally, the purpose of the letters is to commit the church to solidarity with the poor of the land and to defend their interests as pastoral priorities of the church. It is a commitment to renewing its "pastoral service by assuming the struggle for land as the struggle of the God who defends the life of the humble," as expressed in the letter from Panama. Each letter calls for specific actions according to its own context. In general, the bishops delineate four areas for ministry: 1) support for peasant popular organization; 2) direct defense of the land rights of the poor; 3) community-oriented and collective solutions to land problems and injustices; and 4) the direct participation of peasants and indigenous peoples in policy-making concerning land tenancy and rural development.

All the letters emerged from the church's experience of the rural reality. They are intended, in the first instance, to be *pastoral* letters in that they are to orient the church itself. Indeed, the preparation of the letters served to bring the church to a deeper awareness of the problem of land, and to involve many people, clergy as well as lay, in the process. In Chile, for example, over seven hundred peasant groups from all parts of the country participated in preparing the letter. For nearly two years, Catholic missioners and laity worked together to write the letter in Panama that their bishop signed.

LAND AND MINISTRY

Certainly these letters have provoked debate on the problem of land and have inspired and legitimized ministries directly related to the defense of the poor of the land.

CATHOLICS AND PROTESTANTS IN PARAGUAY

In Paraguay, for instance, Protestants and Catholics have joined together in an ecumenical organization called Christian Aid Program to defend the rights of the landless, many of them immigrants from Brazil who have been expelled from lands there. Rev. Juan Schvindt, pastor of the Evangelical Church of the Rio de la Plata, explains that the primary task of the Christian Aid Program is "to reach out to the landless and to those who have been swindled trying to obtain land."

"We have defended land invaders on more than one occasion," he said. "We offer them legal services, and health and educational programs."

The Christian Aid Program endeavors to stimulate peasant organization and was instrumental in the creation of the Farmers' Association of Alto Paraná. Along with the Disciples of Christ, in the cities the organization has been involved in defending the rights of urban squatters.[5]

THE GUATEMALAN BISHOPS' LETTER

Few pastoral letters have provoked such public debate and national controversy as the Guatemalan bishops' letter on land published in early 1988. Land, of course, is the basis for the country's extremely unjust social structure, and, until now, has been a tabu subject even for discussion. As an Amerindian peasant said, "There are three words we are prohibited from using: justice, poor, and land." The ruling oligarchy has no intention of even considering adjustments in land tenure. Yet land is the fundamental issue and must be dealt with before the country's many other major problems can be solved.

Land was already on the church's agenda. During the extremely conflictive 1970s, Catholic priests and bishops, sometimes along with Protestant pastors, were involved in defending the rural poor and struggling for land titles. Some dioceses had incorporated land concerns in their social ministries, and land movements rooted in the church had begun to publicize the issue.

In Coban, in Alta Verapaz, a zone especially marked by land conflicts and persecution of the rural poor, the church has employed a full-time lawyer to deal specifically with land questions. He defends squatters, many times before powerful military officials who also claim the land. Much of his legal work is directed toward land titling and the legalization of community boundaries. He also deals with labor questions pertaining to the relationship between large landowners and the peones who work estates. His role is in the context of the diocese's broader ministry of support for peasant organization and defense of the rights of the poor.

Meanwhile in the southern coastal department of Escuintla, charismatic and populist Father Andrés Girón was giving leadership to the Movement for Land (officially the National Association of Peasants for Land). In 1986, Father Girón and sixteen thousand landless farmers marched for five days from Nueva Concepción to Guatemala City demanding land. Since then they have become the scourge of the landed because of the movement's continual invasions of abandoned or unused agricultural estates. The movement organizes the newly taken estates into production cooperatives, and demands that the government buy the land and resell it on favorable terms to the peasants.

Although the church hierarchy avows moral support and shared concern, it is clear that the movement is Father Girón's personal ministry. Indeed, the bishops make very clear that they do not share his methods. But with perhaps one hundred thousand peasants in the ranks of the movement, the church cannot ignore it.

Thus with land already on the agenda, the bishops felt compelled to pronounce an official word from the church. They begin their letter:

> The cry for land is, without any doubt, the strongest, most dramatic and desperate that one hears in Guatemala. It springs from millions of Guatemalan breasts that not only long to possess the land, but to be possessed by the land. These "People of Corn," on the one hand, feel so profoundly identified with their furrows, planting, and harvesting, and on the other see themselves expelled from the land and prevented from submerging themselves among the fertile furrows by a situation of injustice and sin.
>
> They are as strangers in the land that for millenniums belonged to them, and are considered as second-class citizens in the nation that their colossal ancestors forged.
>
> Perhaps no other theme than that of land tenancy awakens such inflamed passions and provokes such radical and irreconcilable attitudes. But it is a theme that must be faced, if we want to resolve, at least in part, the great problems that afflict us.

What the bishops want, they say, is "serene and profound" reflection on a very "thorny theme," illuminated by God's word, in order "to build a better homeland."

The letter clearly lays out the rural reality of "poverty and misery" that characterizes the life of campesinos:

> The undeniable reality is that the immense majority of the cultivable land is in the hands of a numerically insignificant

minority, while the majority of peasants do not possess even a small piece to cultivate.

And this situation, far from nearing a solution, every day becomes harder and more painful. Certainly the grave problem of land tenancy is the base of our unjust situation.

The bishops review the history of land in Guatemala, and then demonstrate the unequal distribution of agricultural land, using data from the government's 1979 agricultural census. There follows an ample discussion of the social and political consequences of the agrarian structure. They conclude their analysis pointing to the increasing rural violence as "an undeniable fact" rooted in the agrarian structure itself.

The theological section presents land as God's gift to be joyously shared by all. Land is the sign of God's covenant. Those who concentrate land, thus excluding "the poor and helpless," are denounced by the prophets. Then recalling St. James, the bishops affirm that "this denouncement of greed and excessive wealth gained by concentrating land and paying unjust salaries, also is repeated in the New Testament." Jesus becomes poor "in order to realize his mission." As the poor one, Jesus calls the rich to accept their own responsibility for the poor, requiring those who wish to follow him to put "their goods at the service of the needy." Finally, the paschal mystery of Christ transforms the whole of creation, and puts the earth and its resources at the service of the human family.

The letter also reviews how land was understood by the early theologians of the church. "These Bible teachings about the possession of land were amply studied since the beginning of the church. The saints have left us an impressively rich thought and example." The early church's thinking emphasizes the social function of land and that its use should benefit all. The bishops also note that Pope John Paul II in Recife, Brazil, said:

The land is a gift of God, a gift given to all human beings, men and women, those God unites in a single family and draws together with community spirit. It is not licit, therefore, because it does not conform to God's design, to use this gift in such a way that it benefits only a few, leaving others, the immense majority, excluded.

The letter concludes with "pastoral orientations," examining issues related to "integral development" and the "urgency for social structural change" to achieve justice. Most of the specific recommendations relate to the nation's legal system and titling process. Finally they voice a firm no to violence as a means for change, calling instead for change to be forged within "the framework of legality."

Nowhere does the letter mention "agrarian reform," but no one doubted that it was what the bishops intended.

The nation's landowners responded immediately. They pictured the bishops as simplistic and not knowing what they were talking about. They paid for radio announcements explaining that land reform meant stealing land from honest, hard-working people. "Besides," the vice-president of UNAGRO, the organization representing the largest landed and agribusiness interests, explained, "in Guatemala agrarian reform is carried out every day, but within the framework of free enterprise. People sell land when they aren't making a profit, and it passes to other hands."[6]

Another commentator explained, "It's dangerous to resolve earthly problems with heavenly concepts. The problem isn't to take from the one who has a lot," he ventured, "but to give the opportunity for progress to the one who has nothing. The great problem isn't how much land each has, but how one lives. We are dealing with offering all Guatemalans greater equality of opportunity, but maintaining inequality of destiny," he concluded.[7]

Later the landowners sponsored several "technical" studies. Using an impressive array of statistics and graphs, and using the United States as an example, they endeavored to demonstrate the unfeasibility—and nonnecessity—of agrarian reform.

The cry is not for land, they argue, but "for a better life." Using free market economics they conclude:

The pressure to obtain land ought to be understood in the context of the demands of the rural population to reach higher levels of welfare. . . . Development ought to be integral, offering options for progress . . . but the impact on general development would be greater if agrarian policy were founded on respect for *private property* and the utilization of the *market* as the self-regulating mechanism. That would essentially constitute a true *agrarian reform* that would convert agriculture into the motor of development. . . . The marrow of the social problematic, then, is not the absence of an egalitarian distribution of land, but the lack of sufficient sources of stable and well-paid jobs.[8]

The bishops themselves struggled for agreement. It took a year and a half and three drafts before they were able to reach consensus. They had to avoid the tabu words "agrarian reform." The president of the bishops' conference, Rodolfo Quesada Toruño, even denied they were talking about agrarian reform. "What we propose is an intermediate solution," he said.[9] They settled for little steps — "practical things," a bishop explained — that pointed toward solutions.

Yet the letter is prophetic, signaling a real situation. It comes out of lived, pastoral experience, not statistics and economics books. It provokes awareness and debate.

Above all, it puts land squarely on the church's pastoral agenda. It gives legitimacy to pastoral agents long involved in land issues, and stimulates new involvements. The church's moral authority sides with the landless, and cuts away the prohibition of talking about justice, the poor, and the land.

The letter is an instrument for the grassroots to take and use, to study and organize.

CONCLUSION

Pastoral de la tierra — ministry from the land — is now an established ministerial concern for the Latin American church. Still in various ways it is an emerging theme. Other than the pastoral letters themselves, little has been written seeking to define and theologize such a land ministry. Unlike other theological and pastoral concerns, few international meetings have been held to share experiences and discuss the issue of land. Most rural ministries do not incorporate a direct concern for land. In truth, there are few models to follow. The Brazilian church is the pioneering exception and is the topic of the following chapter.

CHAPTER 5

The Brazilian Church and the Struggle for Land

The clearest and most systematic effort to deal with land as a justice issue is in Brazil. Indeed, the concept of land issues as a specific pastoral concern was conceived in Brazil, where it was given the name *pastoral da terra* — ministry from the land. Growing out of the extremely conflictive situation of Brazil's countryside, land justice has emerged as a pastoral priority, with the church as the principal driving force behind efforts to obtain land tenure policies that benefit the poor of the land.[1]

PASTORAL LETTER ON LAND

In 1980 the Catholic Bishops' Conference published the landmark pastoral letter entitled "The Church and the Problem of Land." "Moved by the gospel and by the grace of God," the bishops wrote, "we must not only hear, but assume the sufferings and anguishes, the struggles and hopes, of the victims of unjust distribution and possession of land." After analyzing Brazil's agrarian reality, especially land tenure, the document denounces the unjust pattern of land possession, particularly the concentration of land in the hands of a few wealthy individuals and large corporations. Government policies that favor land concentration are condemned, as is the use of land for speculation and strictly commercial, export-oriented production, at the cost of expelling small landholders and prohibiting access to land by the landless poor. The letter specifically affirms the right of small farmers and Amerindians to land and commits the church to: 1) analyze its own land holdings; 2) denounce injustices related to land; 3) support rural organization and popular initiatives for securing land; and 4) support land reform and the mobilization of Amerindians and small farmers to obtain it. Throughout the document, the condemnation of agrarian capitalism is clear, as is the insistence that land use is legitimized only by its social function.

The document perhaps can be criticized for its apparent contradiction of affirming the right of peasants to have land, and at the same time condemning agrarian capitalism,[2] or for choosing the classic Roman Catholic position of a "third way" between capitalism and socialism, or for not clearly defining new land tenure patterns. Nevertheless, as Dom Pedro Casaldáliga has pointed out, "it is an incalculable stimulus for the struggle of rural workers ... to liberate land and to work the land."[3] It is a profoundly original and prophetic document that commits the church to a very different kind of relationship to the land and to the poor of the land. Dom Paulo Evaristo Arns of São Paulo has indicated very clearly this new position:

> Land is a gift of God. ... In Brazil the church assumed the commitment to denounce openly unjust situations and violence that is committed in diocesan areas. Consequently it will support rural people's efforts for an authentic land reform and the mobilization of workers themselves to demand the application or reformulation of existing laws.[4]

INSTITUTIONAL RESPONSES

This new relationship is expressed through two principal institutional responses: the Pastoral Commission on Land (CPT), and the Missionary Indigenist Council (CIMI). Both grew out of the church's pastoral concern "to do something"[5] about the tremendous inequity in land tenure and, particularly, the tragic and growing violence committed against landless farmers and Amerindian tribals.

In 1975 concerned bishops, priests, and other church workers met in Goiânia "to trace the basic lines for practical pastoral attitudes, to face the latent and existing conflict between agribusiness and landless farmers, as well as the phenomenon of internal migrations resulting from these conflicts."[6] The group established the Pastoral Commission on Land to translate their concerns into practical pastoral actions.

The work of the CPT is built around documentation and analysis of the land situation, particularly violence and the monopolization of land by individuals and corporations, and support for landless farmers through leadership training for their rural unions, and legal services in their struggle for land. A particular concern is to provide alternative information about land rights and to put it in popular form so that it can be readily understood by landless farmers, and through seminars help them analyze and understand Brazil's agrarian policies and rural situation. This process is accompanied by well-researched denunciations of injustices practiced against the poor of the land, often earning the CPT the wrath of big landowners and the government.

Growing out of this work is an ongoing process of theological reflection on the "series of questions relating to faith"[7] that emerge from the rural struggle for land. This ongoing theological work focuses especially on rereading the Bible in the context of the rural struggle for land in order to discover biblical roots both to strengthen that struggle as well as to guide the church's pastoral action. A second dimension is the question of faith and political action, especially in situations of violence and class conflict. The third focus is the church's mission in its "collective, global, messianic, and conflictive dimensions,"[8] especially within the rural context.

The CPT is not conceived as a specialized or technical service relating to land questions. Nor does it try to be a movement in itself, much less to substitute or integrate popular rural movements under the tutorship of the Roman Catholic Church, or other "Catholic movements." Rather it seeks to be a service to pastoral workers and to the poor of the land through solidarity with them in their struggles. The CPT also understands itself as an ecumenical organization, actively seeking the participation of Protestants as well as secular groups who share the same concern for rural justice. Methodists and Lutherans particularly have been active in the CPT, especially in the various regional offices where they have held key posts. Although related to the Catholic Bishops' Conference, the CPT is an autonomous institution with its own general assembly, and is free to speak out on issues and to develop its own program. Divided into various regions, each regional office also maintains a degree of autonomy, enabling the CPT to relate quickly and relevantly to local issues. The various dioceses often appoint priests or hire laypersons to work full-time on CPT issues in their areas. Contact is maintained with a network of rural specialists to advise the CPT, giving its documentation and analysis a high degree of credibility.

Although not charged specifically with questions relating to justice and the land, as is the CPT, land is a fundamental concern of the Missionary Indigenist Council (CIMI).

Founded in 1972, CIMI initially sought: 1) to promote pastoral work among native peoples; 2) prepare missionaries for that work; 3) conscientize the Brazilian general public regarding the situation of native peoples; 4) more closely relate Catholic missions to native peoples to the Catholic Bishops' Conference, government institutions, and to other Christian missions; 5) provide judicial services to missionaries to defend native land rights; and 6) plan study encounters about pastoral work among native peoples.

Originally its focus was on missionaries and ways to deepen their ministries. CIMI, however, began to change quickly. Although the original purposes remain, native peoples themselves have become the principal concern. By 1975 CIMI's three fundamental objectives were defined: 1) defense of land rights; 2) defense of cultures; and 3) tribal self-determination.

Two years later CIMI became an adjunct institution of the Catholic Bishops' Conference. Like the CPT, however, it is autonomous and ecumenical in its approach. It maintains a permanent staff of anthropologists and theologians, and a large network of missionaries and other pastoral workers. Like the

CPT its structure is decentralized into various regional offices to denounce more effectively local injustices and influence government policies. Although in frequent conflict with official government policies toward native peoples, CIMI commands a high degree of respect and credibility for its quality analysis and documentation of the situation of Brazil's native population.

Its general assemblies have defined the right to land as CIMI's priority because land is fundamental to both the cultural and physical survival of Amerindian tribals:

> The primary condition for indigenous communities to reconquer their right to self-determination is possession of land, necessary for their sustenance and sacred for their way of life.
>
> We confirm that all acts of repression and violence against indigenous communities are intrinsically tied to aggression against their lands.[9]

Paulo Suess, a major policy maker and former executive director of CIMI, expresses this priority:

> The question of land is the knot in which all questions about the life of indigenous peoples converge. ... The defense of land forms part of evangelization itself. Solidarity with indigenous peoples over the questions of land is part of anthropological responsibility and pastoral credibility of the missionary. Every official indigenist policy, such as emancipation, aculturation, civilization, integration, must be evaluated in terms of their prejudicial effects on indigenous people's land.[10]

In conclusion Suess writes that defending tribal land rights is the sine qua non of pastoral work among indigenous peoples.[11]

ROMERIAS FOR LAND

This social justice concern for the land rights of the poor is expressed pastorally and liturgically in the many *romerias*, pilgrimages or popular religious marches organized around the theme of land. Here the religious, political, and cultural dimensions of concern for land merge. An average of thirty *romerias* for land occur annually in Brazil and their number is increasing. Participation in them is massive; it is not uncommon for nearly two hundred buses to bring the marchers from the surrounding areas to the starting point.

Under banners large and small calling for land reform and other concerns for rural justice, the several hundred marchers finally end up at a church or religious sanctuary. There, there will be speeches by rural leaders, poetry readings, musical presentations, singing, and praying, along with lots of cold drinks and food. Finally the day's activity will end with a massive celebration of the eucharist and blessing of farm products and tools. As an observer has noted:

> The *romeria* is the moment in which the people confront their reality, their lives, with the reality lived by the People of God — as told in the Bible — and with God's project for the people. It also gives the opportunity for the people to realize that their interests for better life conditions coincide with the will of God.[12]

It is a massive profession of faith, the time to be challenged and inspired as the people are sent forth to continue the struggle for land. "This sending forth or call to personal and collective commitment to the cause of rural workers is never lacking. The farewell is always warm, as are the people themselves."[13]

EXPERIMENTS IN AGRARIAN REFORM

Using its own lands, the church also has experimented with agrarian reform, not only to demonstrate its viability but also to provide models for national land reform. An example is the São Miguel estate in Alagoas.

After many years as a church-owned-and-operated agricultural estate, in 1982 the archdiocese turned over the estate to the peasant workers themselves. A land redistribution program was carried out. It was organized and conducted by the peasant workers themselves, and was based on an evaluation of each family's needs and work possibilities. The families decided to continue paying the rent for use of land as they had always done. However, now the money goes to a community fund they themselves control for community needs such as potable water, access roads, a school teacher's salary, and assistance to families with special needs. The estate's administration is conducted by an elected board and community assemblies.

The transformation of the estate rests on three fundamental points: 1) in addition to land assigned for the private use of each family, some lands are designated for the community's benefit; 2) all major decisions are made collectively; and 3) the basic objective is to benefit everyone equally. An evaluation of the São Miguel experience "showed the great importance that an agrarian reform has, in the sense of bettering the life of rural workers and how, even as a pioneering experience, it obtained results that could be extended to the rest of society."[14]

PROTESTANTS AND THE LAND

Although few Protestants are concerned with land justice, the Evangelical Church of Lutheran Confession of Brazil (IECLB) is an important exception. The IECLB maintains an active missionary presence to tribals and has made the defense of tribal land rights a major aspect of its work. The church continually stresses land and the whole agrarian question as a central theme for study and meditation. Its pastors and other workers are involved actively in both the CPT and CIMI. These workers also have taken a particularly active role in the Movement of Landless Rural Workers, an organization of small farmers based in southern Brazil, the Lutheran Church's stronghold. They have either lost land or are in danger of losing land.

Another specifically Protestant concern for land issues is the Evangelical Commission for Land Rights (CEDITER) of the United Presbyterian Church in Brazil's poor northeast state of Bahia. Established in 1980, CEDITER lawyers provide legal services to small farmers and an educational program for rural unions emphasizing legal rights, leadership training, and theological reflection. Its director, Rev. João Dias, explains that its "objectives are practical, giving support to rural workers and squatters, strengthening rural organization and mobilization." CEDITER also is very interested in theological reflection from the perspective of the landless.

The Ecumenical Service Coordinator (CESE), a large service organization based among Protestants in the northeast, also understands land as a major justice concern. Its staff is deeply involved in land rights issues and the national campaign for land reform. Through its programs it provides various kinds of assistance in defense of land for the rural poor.

Likewise the small Evangelical Missionary Working Group (GTME) seeks to coordinate the pastoral work of Methodists, Anglicans, Lutherans, and Presbyterians among Amerindians and serves as a forum for their missionaries. Like CIMI, with which it works closely, it understands land as fundamental to the survival of Amerindian tribals.

The Ecumenical Center for Documentation and Information (CEDI), with headquarters in Rio de Janeiro, is an important and influential ecumenical effort that serves church and popular movements. Founded in 1974, with strong Protestant participation, it maintains close ties to the World Council of Churches. Through program areas dealing specifically with Brazil's Amerindian tribes and small farmers, CEDI focuses much of its work on land justice issues. It provides program advisers to churches and popular movements. Its documentation of the rural situation is an important source of information for those struggling for fundamental changes in land tenure policies.

DAILY PASTORAL WORK

The most significant response to land justice is the daily pastoral work of countless priests, nuns, pastors, and other church workers. They denounce every injustice. They work with rural unions and community organizations, training leaders and providing legal services to defend the rights of the poor. They help communities recover traditions and struggles, and celebrate victories and defeats with liturgical and biblical symbols. They lead Bible studies, and help groups retell their own histories and interpret those histories in light of the biblical tradition. Above all they keep hope alive not by doing anything special but through simple solidarity with the poor and their struggles.

The church is the only major obstacle that the government and powerful business interests and big landowners must take seriously. So seriously do they take the church, they do everything possible to eliminate it. Persecution is a reality for Christians involved in land issues in Brazil.

THE COST OF DEFENDING THE POOR OF THE LAND

Over the years since 1964 when the military government decided to open Brazil's vast interior for "development," a pattern of calculated repression and intimidation by the large landowners, with the open support of the authorities from the local units of the federal and military police to the president of the republic, has emerged.

Priests, pastoral agents, and other church-related workers have been harassed, interrogated for their supposed communist links, accused of "subversion" and of "inciting" the landless poor to invade the large estates. They have been imprisoned, tortured, expelled from the country, some killed. Bishops have been called to Brasilia to "explain" their priests and to be told to leave the poor of the land alone. As bishops, their consecrations have been challenged, their personal integrity impuned, and their physical well-being threatened and abused. Church agencies, such as the CPT, similarly are attacked. Federal police search their offices and carry off files and educational material deemed "subversive." Authorities and their thugs torment church-sponsored community gatherings and break up special celebrations. These events, so identified with the military dictatorship, continue even with democracy.

Conflict between the landowners and the church is not confined to any one part of Brazil, but it is particularly evident in the northeast, north, and west, the great Amazon basin. Much of this area was opened in the early 1970s, initially designated for large-scale cattle ranching and later for mining, lumbering, and a host of other interests including hydroelectric development. Lucrative fiscal incentives were offered, and wealthy industrialists from the affluent São Paulo and southern regions began to move in.

No one held title to the land, although the region was already populated by Amerindians and *posseiros* or squatters, the small homesteaders who had been expelled from their lands in other parts, particularly the northeast. The government simply ignored them. Instead, it parceled out huge chunks of jungle to rich and powerful cronies and agribusinesses. The ensuing conflicts between the powerful and the poor of the land exploded into tragic proportions that still characterize the region. Early on, the government and the landowners decided that priests must not stand in the way of agribusiness and Brazil's "development."

In 1985 Ezechiele Ramin, a 32-year-old Italian missionary, had been ministering in the far western state of Rondônia for two years. In that brief time, however, he had become known for his commitment to the area's Amerindians and landless poor. Although local landowners had threatened his life, he continued to support the landless. In late July, as he was returning home after a meeting with peasants threatened with expulsion from their homesteads, seven hired gunslingers murdered him.

Reflecting on Father Ramin's murder, a friend said:

Ezechiele's death was not accidental. It was the consequence of a clear and radical option to stand on the side of the oppressed and the dispossessed. The stance was risky. While he clearly did not choose death, the way he lived was disconcerting to those who inhabit the world of violence. And Ezechiele knew that. So they got rid of him.

His death is a challenge to those who still believe in justice. And other courageous people will surely take up that challenge.[15]

Father Josimo Moraes de Taveres did. As regional coordinator for the CPT in the highly conflictive Tocontins area in the central northeast, for several years the 33-year-old Brazilian priest had resolutely demonstrated the church's commitment to the landless. In 1984 he had been arrested on trumped-up charges involving his work with squatters and Amerindians. His life had been threatened on more than one occasion.

Violence against those who struggled for land, and those who defended their right to do so, was an everyday reality. In April

1985, Sister Adelaide Molinari had been murdered in Marabá, when a hired gunman fired at a rural labor leader, hitting her "by mistake."

Looking at his experience and that of numerous other church workers and rural leaders, Father Josimo, as he was simply called, told his pastoral colleagues during their diocesan assembly in 1986:

> All this that is happening is a logical consequence resulting from my work in the struggle and defense of the poor, in favor of the gospel that caused me to assume it to the ultimate consequences.
>
> My life isn't worth much in view of so many workers murdered, assaulted, thrown off their lands — leaving women and children abandoned, without affection, without bread and without a home.[16]

On May 10, 1986, Father Josimo was shot to death in Imperatriz, Maranhão, by a hired gunman. The murderer later was sentenced to prison, but the landowners who hired him never have suffered legal consequences.

Missionaries working with Indian tribals through CIMI also have suffered persecution. By 1988 sixteen missionaries had been expelled or formally prohibited from entering certain Amerindian areas by the government. The mysterious death of Jesuit Vicente Canas had not been clarified more than a year after his body was found in the jungles of Mato Grosso. An autopsy report showed that he had died of physical aggression.[17]

Violence and repression against the church, however, are not limited to Roman Catholics, nor to the vast Amazon basin. United Presbyterian pastors have had their lives threatened for defending the poor of the land, and Methodists have been arrested for participating in demonstrations by the landless.

Protestant pastors also are murdered. Baptist minister José Inácio da Silva Filho, 58, was pastor in Timon, nearly five hundred kilometers north of São Luis, Maranhão. Rev. da Silva Filho was well known for the support he gave to the struggle of squatters and other landless poor. He had been accused by the big landowners of inciting the poor to invade their properties.

In May 1986 he too was shot to death, as he was leaving his home for church. According to his family, he had received death threats, and local police said his murder was ordered by the area's big landowners, or possibly he was confused with someone else.[18]

The IECLB, the Protestant denomination best known for its commitment to land rights and the poor, has been harassed continually. Its missionaries have been expelled from their remote posts when their defense of Amerindian land rights became too much for powerful economic interests. Lutheran pastors have been arrested and sent to jail for publicly denouncing the army, government, landowners, and others who exploit the poor and take their lands. Their solidarity with the Movement of Landless Rural Workers, especially in the southern part of the country, has been a source of constant conflict with agrointerests and governmental authorities.

A HISTORY OF VIOLENCE AGAINST THE CHURCH

This history of repression against the church dates from before the 1980s. In 1967 in the Santa Terezinha area of southern Pará and northern Mato Grosso, the French priest Father François Jentel began working the Tapirapé Indians and peasant squatters. He especially was concerned for their land rights and sought to secure legal titles. By 1972 the homesteaders were engrossed in deep conflict with a land company owned by a large São Paulo bank. Father Jentel was blamed for the conflict and accused of being a communist subversive. He was arrested and sentenced to ten years in prison by a military court. However, the lone civilian judge dissented, saying that Father Jentel "deserves a prize, not prison."[19] Father Jentel later was expelled from Brazil.

Santa Terezinha is part of the diocese of São Felix do Araguaia, whose bishop is the indomitable Dom Pedro Casaldáliga. Bishop Casaldáliga already had problems with landowners and military authorities. The day he was consecrated bishop, in 1971, he released a clandestinely published pastoral letter in which he described the plight of squatters and Amerindians before the onslaughts of the big landowners. He named the corporations and the owners, and spelled out the injustices they committed. Following Father Jentel's arrest, the military took over São Felix, arresting the pastoral team and other workers in church programs. The parish house was ransacked and files carried off. The same thing happened simultaneously in other villages of the prelature. A smear campaign accusing Bishop Casaldáliga of being a communist agitator was launched and continued for many years.

A Brazilian Jesuit, Father João Bosco Penido Burnier also was well known for his defense of the poor of the land, especially the Bakairi Amerindians with whom he worked as a missionary and regional coordinator for CIMI. In October 1976, while traveling with Bishop Casaldáliga to Ribeirão Bonito, some eight hours south of São Felix, he was murdered by the police. The sister and the daughter-in-law of a local squatter were being held hostage in the village's jail. The two priests were seeking their release when an angered policeman shot Father João Bosco in the face.

To the south of Ribeirão Bonito, the Bororo Amerindians live on a reserve, in eastern Mato Grosso. Their once extensive territory has been reduced to only a fraction of what it formerly was. In the early 1970s the Salesian Fathers, particularly Father Rudolph Lunkenbein, director of the mission station at Meruri, were defending the Amerindians' right to their land and protested intrusions to public authorities. Father Lunkenbein urged the legalization of their lands in order to avoid serious conflict. In July 1976 a carload of drunken and angry landowners arrived at the Meruri mission station. They shouted angrily for Father Lunkenbein. When he appeared, he was shot to death along with an Amerindian who rushed to his aid. Four others were wounded in the wild shooting spree. Although well known, the killers were never arrested.

The São Geraldo do Araguaia region, some four hundred kilometersnorth of São Felix and part of the Conceição do Araguaia diocese, has been especially conflictive. By the mid-1970s the church increasingly was concerned about the violence committed against the landless farmers, and the systemic injustice that denied them land to work but seemed to guarantee huge estates to wealthy businessmen. In 1976 the church began providing legal services to a group of São Geraldo squatters to aid them in their struggle to obtain land titles.

Three years later Father Aristides Camio and his recently arrived colleague, Father Francois Gouriou, were deeply involved in providing pastoral services to the landless farmers, and aiding them in their struggle for land. The zone was militarized due to the conflict between landowners and squatters, and the two priests were singled out as the causes of the ensuing violence.

Their arrest by military authorities began one of the most celebrated trials in the history of the Brazilian church. They were charged under the vague national security law with "inciting collective disobedience of the law," and "inciting violent class struggle."

The trial by military court was held in Belem, June 21–22, 1982. Thirteen Roman Catholic bishops and various Protestant observers were present. In the streets outside the courtroom, hundreds of Christians demonstrated in support of the priests. Nearly two thousand military police sought to keep "order."

By a 4 to 1 vote of the judges, Father Camio was condemned to fifteen years in prison, and Father Gouriou to ten. The church was shocked. No evidence ever was presented to back up the charges. Even the most conservative of Brazil's bishops recognized the injustice. Finally, after having served two-and-a-half years in prison, their sentences were declared completed and they were released.

Through the years, most of the violence has fallen upon the church's lay workers, and active Catholic rural leaders. They have been imprisoned and murdered for their struggle for justice in the land. They too, are martyrs of the church.

Violence against the church in Brazil is neither isolated nor by chance. It is, rather, a calculated effort to eliminate the church's pastoral concern for the poor of the land. It seeks to isolate peasant farmers and Amerindians from those who express solidarity with them, and falls particularly upon the church because it is the church, above other institutions, that has identified with the cause of the landless.

The Brazilian Benedictine monk and theologian Marcelo Barros Souza, following the death of Father Josimo, clearly identified the church's solidarity with the poor of the land with the cross of Jesus Christ:

> In the case of Father Josimo and so many other martyrs of the land, the cross is no longer a physical thing that one can be tied to and hung on. The cross upon which Josimo and our martyrs of the land are dying is the same cross that we ought to take and carry in our struggle. This cross, very concretely, is called, in Brazil, Agrarian Reform.[20]

But the significance of persecution is not in suffering itself. The significance is the breaking forth of new creation, the resurrection, that persecution births. The cross and resurrection cannot be separated. Together they are the seedbeds of hope and justice, the basis for pastoral work. Father Camio's and Father Gouriou's bishop, Dom Patrick Joseph Hanrahan of Conceição do Araguaia, reflecting upon their experience, said, "it is the cross of Jesus Christ that must guide us, and it is the resurrection that we must announce, whatever it costs."

CONCLUSION

Perhaps as no other issue, land has consumed the Brazilian church. Christians have assumed a fundamental role in the defense of land rights for the rural poor and are the principal movers seeking new land tenure policies. The church has developed particular institutional expressions of that concern and incorporated the concern for land into its daily ministry. It takes considerable risks and has suffered greatly for its solidarity. Indeed, pressures to curb its commitment to the poor of the land have even come from within the church itself. International church funding agencies have limited funding of the CPT.

Perhaps more significantly, the conservative mood of the Vatican brought about in 1988 the silencing for an indefinite period of Dom Pedro Casaldáliga. Undoubtedly Dom Pedro, as everyone calls him, is the Brazilian church's most outspoken bishop in defense of the landless, and most identified with the CPT. As another Brazilian bishop said, "Sadly, all that the military regime was unable to do against Dom Pedro during twenty years, the church itself is doing now, with the silencing."[21] But no other church in Latin America has confronted the tragic reality of land like the Brazilian Catholic Church. In all, it offers a pastoral model that inspires the whole church in Latin America as it too struggles for justice in the land.

CHAPTER 6

Land and Ministry

The possession and use of land in Latin America cannot be marginal to the church's ministry. As we have seen, land not only is a fundamental biblical theme, but is the basis for grave injustices committed against the poor of the land even today. We must take the theme of land as the prism[1] for understanding present socio-historic reality and for founding a ministry that will make "promised land," with all its implications for social transformation, a reality. In the contemporary Latin American context, that promise is given to peasants, small farmers, and Amerindians. That recognition implies explicit pastoral intervention in the struggle for and defense of their lands.

Today, as in ancient Israel, land pertains to the essence of the present and future of peasant and Amerindian peoples. "Land-life-future" continues to be an inseparable unity. Without land, peasants and Amerindians have nothing. Land means future and, for them, salvation. The identification of land with salvation can be explicit. As a Mexican peasant said following a conflict with a large landholder, "Jesus saves me when they give me land." Or, as another said, "For me, salvation is to be able to leave a little piece of land to my children." In Honduras, after receiving a plot of marginal land through the nation's land reform agency, peasant farmers explained, "at last we are free!"

It was the first time in their lives to have their own land. For them it meant freedom from being exploited day laborers. It meant they no longer had to go about "working here and there," as one said.

For the rural poor, land—soil for cultivation and territory for living—is promise and salvation, identity and divine presence, sustenance and power over their own lives. It always means security, because their "portion" is still understood as inheritance, not as a consumer item. It becomes a "consumer item" only when pressures from big landowners force them to "sell" in the context of policies that seek to eliminate the small landholder. To preach "the poor shall inherit the earth" makes sense only in this socio-historic context.

TOWARD MINISTRY FROM THE LAND

Pastoral action must deal with issues of ministry and ethics as they relate to the ownership, use, and maintenance of land. Specifically, a ministry from the land must seek socio-economic arrangements that will ensure just and secure access to land for the rural poor and use practices that assure the well-being of all people, especially the poor. It must be politico-pastoral action because fundamentally it will be about altering the structure of power based on land ownership, and ultimately the structure of power within the whole socio-political order. It also must involve an essential process of theological and ideological reflection for understanding the meaning of the struggle for land and envisioning an ecologically sound new society characterized by love, justice, and well-being. As ministry, although related to other pastoral concerns such as social promotion through agricultural development and rural work in general, it has its own specificity because of its concern to effect essential structural changes. Thus it is ministry that is unavoidably conflictive and controversial.

THE CHURCH AND JUSTICE IN THE LAND

A U.S. farm activist has observed regarding the church and the family farm crisis in North America:

The church is called to overcome decades of neglect to bring to the struggle a number of its gifts: a renewed and renewing understanding of the covenantal community of the people of God on the God-given land; a prophetic voice raising the challenge of distributive justice on the land; an activist stance with those who organize and empower rural people; a clear presence in the public policy arena to develop and secure just farm, food, and land policies; and its full prophetic, economic, and political strength to challenge and transform the corporate and financial powers that would continue to dominate life on the land.[2]

His observation is equally appropriate as the church seeks to be in mission to the poor of the land in Latin America. Indeed each of the points he raises is fundamental to the church's mission in Latin America.

Seeking more specifically the "content" of the church's mission to the poor of the land, we are guided by at least six fundamental ethical principles regarding justice in the land. They emerge from the biblical tradition:

1) Land is a gift to sustain human life; nevertheless, human action is required to secure it and to establish justice.

2) Land is for all people because it is the source of life; its use, therefore, is legitimated by its social, not private, function.

3) Since land pertains to all, it is to be distributed in the context of the jubilee-reign of God; the organizing principle is *koinonia.*

4) Land is not to be coveted or concentrated; all must have access to the land.

5) Land itself is to be respected, allowed to "rest," so that it will produce for the benefit of all; ecological destruction is prohibited.

6) Those who work the land must be duly and fairly compensated; exploitation of laborers is not permitted.

These six interrelated principles are the guidelines for pastoral activity.

Land is a gift to sustain life; nevertheless, human action is required to secure it and to establish justice. In the first instance, ministry must be oriented toward securing and defending land, and establishing just ownership and labor patterns. Strengthening the organizations of peasant farmers and indigenous peoples is of fundamental importance. Only through strong unionlike organizations will they be able to instigate actions for obtaining land or defending the land they already have. Since the protagonists of the struggle for land are popular movements, pastoral work must express itself in solidarity with them. This implies that pastoral work must stimulate the poor of the land to organize and must be involved in such integrally related activities as leadership training and conscientization.

It also means orienting the poor of the land to their rights before existing laws as well as the theological significance of "promised land" in their actual socio-political context. Of special importance is facilitating legal counsel to peasants, Amerindians, and small farmers, and launching legal actions on their behalf. Rural development programs, for example, could include legal advisers as permanent staff, available to peasant and indigenous people's organizations for the defense of their lands.

At the same time, research and data collection and interpretation from the perspective of the poor of the land is fundamental. Put in popular form and placed at the disposal of the poor, such information can be a major resource for their struggle. Likewise it is information that lawyers use, that forms public opinion and the basis for international pressures. Finally, it is such information that backs up denunciations of injustices.

This particularly is urgent on the international level. The churches must educate their own First World constituencies about the consequences of their own government's economic and foreign aid policies and those of international financial institutions, as well as the private policies of transnational businesses, on the lives of the Latin American poor and their lands.

The prophetic voice that denounces every injustice and violence against the poor of the land is an essential part of ministry related to land and must be raised not only in Latin America, but also in the centers of world power. Its purpose is to secure justice and promote lasting and fundamental changes in the dominant economic model and power structure. This can be achieved only with international solidarity.

Land is for all people because it is the source of life; its use, therefore, is legitimated by its social, not private, function. Fundamentally land is not for private gain but to produce for basic human needs, both physical and existential. Ministry must concern itself with agricultural policies that are oriented toward producing adequate food resources for all, especially the poorest. All rural development programs—water resource development, types of agricultural production, economic scale, technological inputs—as well as the overall economic and agricultural policies of a nation, must be judged in terms of the social benefits produced, measured by the degree to which the poorest sectors benefit, not the private benefits that accrue to a minority.

Again, this is not just a local issue. It transcends national boundaries not only because international agencies are involved, but also because policies adopted to serve the needs of one country can be detrimental to the poor in another. For example, the fundamental purpose of U.S. food aid to poor countries is to provide a market for U.S. farm surplus production. That is good for U.S. farmers. But food aid often serves as a disincentive to national food production by driving down local prices, thus adversely affecting peasant farmers who produce their country's basic grains. Likewise, the "comparative advantage" law that urges poor countries to end basic grain production in favor of export commodities, and instead to import basic foodstuffs from the U.S.A. and Europe because they are cheaper, simply means that the problem of U.S. and European farmers is solved by destroying small farmers in Latin America. Solutions must be sought in their global, not local, context.

Evaluation of policies and programs also must include the impact of such development programs on lands that are "homes," both physically and symbolically. This is particularly important for Amerindian tribals whose sense of home is related integrally to their lands, both physically and existentially. Indeed, as explained in previous chapters, for both peasant and tribal societies, home and work are integrated, not differentiated as autonomous activities. Thus land as home implies not only a place to live, but personal identity and sustenance as well.

Since land pertains to all, it is to be distributed in the context of the jubilee-reign of God; the organizing principle is koinonia. Sharing and solidarity are fundamental to the Christian faith, so much so that early Christians sought to organize their lives, including property relations, around them. The term several New Testament writers chose to express these essential concepts is *koinonia*. It is used, in its various forms, nearly forty times, particularly in Acts, the Pauline literature, and 1 John. The Gospel writers express the same concepts but in other forms. The word itself can be translated in various ways: communion and community, participation and fraternity, unity and union, sharing and contribution. Basically it means to share something with someone in a deep sense of solidarity. *Koinonia* also contains both a spiritual and historical dimension related dialectically. *Koinonia* as spiritual reality always expresses itself historically. Thus the collection for the poor of Jerusalem is *koinonia* (Rom. 15:26); the sharing community in Jerusalem is *koinonia* (Acts 2:24, 42–47; 4:32–51).

For early Christians who heard Jesus' reign of God preaching, *koinonia* exemplified their new life in Christ expressed in terms of their various relationships. It was a way of living, characteristic of those who received God's saving grace. God initiated *koinonia* and called Christians to live *koinonia* (1 Cor. 1:9; Phil. 2:1; 2 Cor. 13:4). Not to have lived *koinonia* would have been a contradiction of the gospel itself. It was a way of living eschatologically. As they hopefully awaited the end of time and Jesus' triumphant return, they created their own common life as a live reflection of the expected future. The eschatological future dawned in the historical present as a sign of God's reign. *Koinonia* inevitably implied an alternative social model.

The community of goods among Jerusalem Christians is illuminating (Acts 2:42–47; 4:32–51). Although we are told very little about the community and apparently it did not prosper as the dominant form of *koinonia* among early Christians (and certainly not later ones), it remains an important model with contemporary implications.

Studying the passage in Acts 4, four aspects of that community can be distinguished:
1. profound spiritual communion (v. 32);
2. a classless society (v. 34);

3. renunciation of private property (v. 32);
4. a community of economic goods (v. 32).

Those Jerusalem Christians hardly envisioned their community as a historical project. However, *koinonia* makes sense only as it assumes historical shape informing a new socio-economic model, again as a sign of God's reign. At the very least it implies the radical questioning of capitalist relations in terms of property and the means of production. It would suggest that the church is called to struggle for a socio-economic model characterized by:

1. profound community;
2. classless social organization;
3. renunciation of capitalist property and social relations;
4. community-based economic resources and means of production.

Land, then, cannot be a capital good, transferable as a consumer item for strictly individual financial gain. Rather what ethically is required is *secure access* to land. The fundamental question is not private, capitalist ownership, but arrangements that assure use of the land within the context of *koinonia*. This suggests that land ownership patterns need to be analyzed and distinguished.

In their pastoral letter on land, the Brazilian Catholic bishops usefully distinguish between "land for exploitation" and "land for working":

> *Land for exploitation* is land that capital continually appropriates in order to always generate new and growing profits. Those profits equally come from the exploitation of the labor of those who lost their land and their work tools, or who never had access to land, as well as speculation that permits the enrichment of some at the cost of the total society.

Land for exploitation is capitalist property in which land itself is transferable capital and where the relationship for making it produce is private enterprise for personal gain.

> *Land for working* is land possessed by the one who works it. It is not land for exploiting others nor for speculation.

In our country [Brazil] the concept of land for working appears most clearly in the popular right to family, tribal, or community property, which gives right to possession. These forms of property, alternatives to capitalist exploitation, clearly open a wide road that makes viable communitarian labor even in extensive areas and the utilization of adequate technology, making alien exploitation unnecessary.

It is worthwhile to distinguish between capitalist land, and the private property of land. While the first is utilized as an instrument for exploiting alienated labor, the second is used as a tool for personal and family labor.

Land for working, although private, is not a transferable, capital good that can be exchanged at will for personal gain.[3] Nor is its production based on the exploitation of labor other than personal, family, community, or collective effort.

As the bishops suggest, it is important to distinguish among modes of ownership and production. Peasant- and tribal-based economies essentially are communitarian, highly integrated economies. They contain many forms of community cooperation that, while the needs of individuals are met, are, at bottom, oriented toward the needs of the whole community. The community maintains much control. Peasant economies and tribal traditions offer rich possibilities. There is no inherent reason why these "primitive" forms cannot serve a productive agriculture. To utilize their essential values is not to return to the past, but to take advantage of values to move forward. Ethically, landownership must be taken out of the framework of capitalist property and oriented toward a community-based economy.

Of course many of the poor of the land are neither peasants nor Amerindians. They are struggling small farmers forced into the capitalist mode of production. With them ministry will concern itself with finding alternative, economically viable forms of landownership and agricultural production that also reflect *koinonia*.[4]

As in Brazil, churches with agricultural estates can experiment with alternative models of possession and use of land. Those models would be prototypes for the whole of society, stimulating other efforts and demonstrating their viability. At the same time they would serve prophetically as an implicit critique of the dominant system.

The guide for seeking just, nonexploitive patterns of land-ownership and land use is *koinonia,* worked out historically. There is no single mode, but it remains the norm. This norm, however, clearly urges significant land reform for social transformation as the basis for a more just social order.

Land is not to be coveted or concentrated; all must have access to the land. This, of course, is implicit in the foregoing discussion of *koinonia.* It is important, however, to recognize that the struggle for land by the poor is not to covet land. There is a qualitative difference in taking land, for instance, as squatters, in order to sustain life, and taking land for ever-increasing profits. The struggle for land by the landless is the struggle for life. It is the struggle to receive from God the gift that is essential to the well-being of their families and communities, and to their futures.

The question of concentration of land, often justified by the concept of "economy of scale," the economic law that large units produce more efficiently and therefore more cheaply than small ones, basically is the question of who has access to land. Concentration necessarily excludes the majority because its lands are "concentrated" in the hands of the few. At the same time, as was discussed in the second chapter, economy of scale is not necessarily better, and certainly does not imply a food-based agriculture for the needs of the poorest social sectors. Indeed, economy of scale raises serious ethical questions around who owns the land and who benefits from its production. Smaller units or socially owned large units more nearly reflect the ethical requirement that land not be coveted or the poor excluded.

Land itself is to be respected, allowed to "rest," so that it will produce for the benefit of all; ecological destruction is prohibited. The purpose of the land is to provide for human need. It is for that reason that humankind was given "dominion" over the earth (Gen. 1:28). Nature was entrusted to the care and management of humankind,[5] for the benefit of the present, as well as future, generations. Later, the land and God's blessing were given not only to a particular patriarch, but "to your descendants forever" (Gen. 13:15, etc.).[6] The gift of the natural order must be passed on so that future generations also might have the resources for life. Therefore:

> Nature is not meant for the selfish and exclusive use of the
> first [person] to come upon a particular piece of it, but is
> to be [cared] for all [people] for all generations. [They]
> live in the context of history and community, and [their]
> decisions regarding nature must be responsible to [their]
> setting. [One] does not enjoy absolute right of disposition
> over natural resources, but is their steward, the caretaker
> of their divine owner, using them and preserving their use-
> fulness to future ages. Of course the biblical writers know
> how rapacious [people] can be. That is why they sternly
> admonish [them] to a right use of the gift of the earth.[7]

The question of ecology—that is, the preservation of the natural order—must be understood in the context of social justice.
Unfortunately, the relationship between environmental concern
and social justice too often is not seen. Many times environmentalists fail to recognize that environmental destruction is
caused by deep social injustices. Peasant squatters may indeed
be burning off the tropical forest, but they do so only because
there has been no meaningful land reform that would give them
access to land. To expel them from natural areas, or otherwise
prohibit them access to forest resources—for instance, to gather
firewood and cut timber for their homes and corrals—can mean
unacceptable hardship, itself as ethically wrong as the destruction of the environment. Likewise many environmentalists fail
to understand that the drive to export, with its consequent environmental destruction, responds particularly to the economic
development model discussed in chapter 2. Furthermore, option
for the model is related directly to the nation's external debt
and economic policies imposed by the world's financial institutions. Without meaningful changes for justice in the social order,
environmental concerns themselves become injustices.

It must not be forgotten that "rest" in the biblical tradition
fundamentally is about justice. Ecological destruction, destroying the resources of life, especially for the poorest social sectors
who cannot escape to clean neighborhoods or uneroded soils,

and whose labor is exploited often under unsanitary and hazardous conditions through the indiscriminate use of pesticides and herbicides, is a social reality "justified" in the name of "progress." However, that destruction is not the fault of the poor, but rather the avarice and selfishness of wealthy developers whose only concern is immediate profit, in which the poor of the land are used as their instruments.

An environmental ethic that is socially just is urgent. For this reason, recognizing the symbiotic relationship between nature and human welfare, especially of the poor, always must have priority. Thus nature cannot be separated from, but rather incorporated into, the sphere of history together with a positive concept of the possibilities of technology and economic growth within the framework of the just distribution of wealth. Nevertheless, a sober and limited anthropocentrism is extremely important, and the "dominion" given to humans is to be understood as stewardship and as a call to live a life that favors others. Thus a socially just environmental ethic requires the recognition that we are obligated to future generations through the just and proper use of resources and possessions.[8]

For these reasons such an ethic strongly questions an economic concept of the use of land and its resources that valorizes private gain. Rather, it requires the use of land and its resources within the context of justice, participation, and sustainability. Justice places emphasis on purpose and destiny—for whom is the land used and for what purpose? As has been said, justice requires that the poor be the primary beneficiaries of the use of land, and that the purpose of use must be to provide for the needs of human welfare both present and future. Participation underlines the aspect of access to power and decision-making by the marginalized and their right to enjoy their citizenship as integral members of society, including use of the land. Sustainability refers directly to ecological limits and implies use practices that assure the permanent productivity of the land, thus guaranteeing a future for coming generations.[9]

Those who work the land must be duly and fairly compensated; exploitation of laborers is not permitted. Exploitive labor practices in Latin American agriculture were discussed in the first chapter. Clearly an ethic for the land requires fundamental changes in labor relations. At the very least, just salaries and social benefits are the right of all agricultural workers. They also have the right to humane working and living conditions, as well as the freedom to leave work as they choose, governed only by mutually agreed upon contractual relations. Moving beyond a strictly management-labor relation, workers should be included in profit-sharing and have opportunities to own company stock, while under conditions of capitalism. They also cannot be denied independent, autonomous union organization for collective bargaining and defense of worker interests. Finally, alternatives to capitalist enterprise, such as worker-owned-and-operated companies, ought to be stimulated.

These ethical guidelines are neither exhaustive nor definitive. They are, rather, generative themes that must provoke critical reflection on ministry that will lead to justice for the poor of the land.

SOLIDARITY AND THE U.S. CHURCHES

The solidarity of Christians in the United States is critical to justice for the poor of the land in Latin America. The guidelines presented in the previous section offer a profile of the "content" of that mission solidarity. In addition, the churches must:

1. Educate their constituencies as to the reality of landlessness in Latin America, why it exists and is increasing, and its social consequences for the poor.

2. Link, as part of a global concern, the struggle of U.S. farmers, Amerindians, and others with the struggles of Latin America's poor of the land.

3. Examine critically the policies of AID, IMF, and the World Bank regarding their implications for the poor of the land, and advocate instead policies that secure access to land and well-being for the poor.

4. Examine critically the ethical and economic implications of U.S. domestic agricultural policy and foreign food assistance for food production and landownership in Latin America, and seek solutions to the U.S. farm crisis that do not prejudice poor farmers in Latin America.

5. Examine critically land reform as part of rural develop-

ment, and support programs that imply not only real access to land by the poor, but also broader social transformation and power restructuring conducive to greater distributive justice.

6. Examine critically the practices of U.S. private corporations regarding land and the poor, and expose and denounce their role in landlessness.

7. Commit church resources to the defense of the land rights of the poor in solidarity with Latin American churches and popular movements.

8. Provide the poor of the land, through the various agencies of the churches, a forum to plead their cause before world opinion.

Although speaking to the churches in reference to North America, again the words of the U.S. rural activist are valid for the churches and their mission to Latin America:

> This is the challenge of the 90s: to confront effectively the power of those interests that would control the land base and the food production and distribution system in this nation and worldwide. The disregard by those powers for the people they displace, the poverty they perpetuate, the underclass they cultivate, is categorically unacceptable.[10]

May the churches respond to this global challenge.

CONCLUSION

Brueggemann reminds us that in their pilgrimage toward the promised land, there are "two histories" active among the people of Israel (Num. 14):

> One is driven by a sense of banishment, characterized by mistrust expressed as quarrelsomeness and is devoted to return to Egypt. The other is the history of hope, trusting in Yahweh's promises, enduring in the face of want and need, sure that history was on its way to a new and good land.[11]

In spite of the desperate situation, still without land, Joshua and Caleb were able to have confidence in the future and to see the presence and power of God, while the others lacked trust and wanted to return. Brueggemann suggests that these attitudes show two ways of understanding landlessness: as a confident journey toward land, or as a despairing road toward definitive landlessness. "The ones who will come to the land are those who have maintained their expectancy and have grown neither weary nor cynical," he writes.[12]

The church's ministry must be a source of confidence and hope for peasants, Amerindians, and small farmers, and all the poor of the land, in their struggle to have land, so that they might not faint and lose the promise. The church must show God's presence among them, as part of their struggle. Finally it must proclaim the message, again as Brueggemann writes, that "Yahweh has taken sides and acts powerfully for the landless, powerfully enough to overcome and defeat the enormous power of those who control land and sit on thrones."[13]

Epilogue

This book has been about land and landlessness in rural Latin America. Landlessness, however, is neither limited to Latin America nor to rural areas. It not only is a serious problem in North America, Africa, and Asia, it is urban as well as rural.

In 1982 the Brazilian Catholic bishops spoke out on the problem of urban land just as they previously spoke out on rural land. In a pastoral letter they analyzed urban land use and its highly unequal distribution. They point specifically to speculation as the major reason why the masses of rural poor pouring in to Brazil's cities find no living space:

> Migration to urban centers coincides with a rapid increase in land values due to intense real estate speculation. Large numbers of empty lots are held for this reason. They amount to about one-third of the space suitable for construction in Brazilian cities. ... By inflating the price of land, real-estate speculation aggravates the country's housing situation. A basic characteristic of urban land use for housing is the unequal distribution among different social strata.

For instance, the bishops indicate that in Rio de Janeiro, "urban land occupied by *favelas* (shantytowns) amounts to less than 10 percent of the city's total land mass. But in that 10 percent live 35 percent of Rio's entire population."

Expelled from the countryside, the poor of the land demand a decent place to live along with basic services, but are forced to live in squalid conditions because no space is available. In desperation they invade any vacant area they can find, often only to be repulsed by police "protecting" private property. However, as the bishops write, "Many fail to realize that land occupation by the migrant population ... is the only solution possible for the impasse in which they find themselves."

The desperate situation of the landless urban poor causes the bishops to conclude that:

> The right to make use of urban land to guarantee adequate housing is one of the primary conditions for creating a life that is authentically human. Therefore when land occupations — or even land invasions — occur, legal judgments on property titles must begin with the right of all to adequate housing. All claims to private ownership must take second place to this basic need.
>
> Bearing in mind the teaching of Pope John Paul II, that all private property carries with it a social responsibility, we conclude that the natural right to housing has priority over the law that governs land appropriation. A legal title to property can hardly be an absolute value in the face of the human need of people who have nowhere to make their home.

Throughout Latin America one finds the same desperate situation of urban landlessness. Land occupations and shantytowns characterize Santiago, Lima, Bogotá, San José, and Mexico City. The problem of land as "habitable space" is the universal problem of the poor.

This problem is not limited to Latin America. In Canada, Amerindians are struggling to retain rights to their traditional territories that the government has opened for natural gas, petroleum, and other mineral exploration. In the United States, the once vibrant middle-class family farms increasingly are being incorporated into lands owned by large businesses, often unrelated to agriculture. In the deep south, black farmers increasingly are alienated from the land. By the turn of the century, U.S. blacks my be totally landless. Farm workers continue to struggle for the right to organize, and Amerindians face powerful mining interests.

In Australia, aborigines are fighting to recover and retain their lands that are being taken by ranchers and mineral and oil companies. Land especially is important to aborigines because their self-identity as human persons is related to specific "sacred sites." Such sites are basic elements in their culture. A sacred site is a peculiar land form or rock formation, together with trees and other natural features. These sacred sites give meaning to life. When the site is destroyed, as by mining, or "injured," as by oil wells, the site "dies," and so do the people, the aborigines. The sacred sites are sources of life. Unfortunately, many sacred sites also are rich mineral deposits coveted by Western mining companies. The struggle to save sacred sites and other lands is related to the very survival of aborigines as a people.

The legacy of colonialism continues to erode traditional lands in Africa for the lucrative export of plantation crops — rubber, African palm, pineapple and other tropical fruits, and cotton; and mineral exploitation — iron, phosphates, zinc, diamonds, manganese, and gold. Yet across the great continent, depending on the vast variety of geographical terrains and climatic conditions, Africa is overwhelmingly a land of subsistence farmers and herders. Most are reduced to tiny plots hardly adequate for subsistence, where they grow peanuts, beans, corn, yams, cassava, and rice. Erosion, deforestation, and overgrazing, coupled with the introduction of commercial crops and disregard for traditional — but ecologically sound and economically viable for subsistence — technology continues to seriously harm their resource base. Throughout ex-colonial tropical Africa, landlessness and insecure tenure provoke rural unrest and violent confrontations, as peasants are marginalized from the land.

South African apartheid forces native blacks off their lands, both urban and rural, to be relocated in "homelands," thus making rich land resources available to whites as well as creating a large reservoir of cheap labor. In the last twenty years, nearly three and a half million people have been "relocated" and some two million more are threatened with forced removal from their lands.

Virtually all South African land is reserved for whites. Blacks who still work the land are labor tenants on white-owned farms. Even though their families may have lived on the same farm for generations, their continued tenancy depends on the goodwill of the white landlord. In return for labor services, the black family receives a small wage and usufruct right to cultivate a portion of the land. They can be evicted without cause or legal process, and thus are able to stay on the land only as long as the family can provide able-bodied labor for the white farmer.

Urban landlessness for blacks also is acute. In fact, homelessness arguably is the most serious social problem in South Africa. It directly affects at least five million people. Because of stringent apartheid laws, blacks are prohibited from living in most areas of urban space. Squatting is the only alternative, but it is illegal. Thus one of six South Africans is without proper shelter or is living illegally somewhere he or she is not supposed to be. Living conditions are poor, and tenure is precarious.

Landlessness is particularly acute in Asia. Studies by the Food and Agriculture Organization (FAO) show that a majority of Asian countries have experienced an alarming increase in landlessness in recent decades.

India is a great producer of basic grains. But the "green revolution" that made it possible, not only has led to greater concentration of farmland, it also has bypassed many areas, hardly benefiting the mass of India's peasantry. Over half the nation's farmers are landless. In numerous areas, peasants continue as feudal serfs.

A journalist has described the eastern state of Bihar as "a time warp of servitude, slavery, starvation, and class warfare."[1] The feudal social order is dominated by large landowners who have absolute power over the masses of peasant harijans or untouchables. Bonded servitude (although illegal) ties the peasant family to the landlord for life, and subjects the family members to humiliation and physical abuse, not only in Bihar but other states also. Land disputes are common and violent.

Bangladesh is one of the poorest countries in the world. Its colonial heritage has left it with an extremely unequal distribution of the land. At least 62 percent of its farmers are landless or near landless. Recent years of modernization have done little to reduce poverty and landlessness.

In Thailand at least two million farm families (some ten million people) own fewer than 2.5 hectares each, while large commercial plantations, many owned by the great transnational fruit companies, effectively dominate the rural economy. Over a half-million people work the plantations, and another half-million are farmers with no access to land. In all, over a third of the farming population is in need of land.

This same story can be told for Indonesia, Philippines, and Malaysia. Indeed, it is the story of the whole region.

Even in South Korea, where land reform forced more equitable land tenure, and policies have benefited small-scale, intensive farming, 67 percent of farm households have no more than one hectare of land. Although aggregate incomes from these farmers has increased, their share in the total economy is deteriorating, especially relative to urban incomes. Among the smallest farmers, only about half of their annual incomes can be earned in agriculture; the rest must be made as laborers and peddlers. About 90 percent of South Korean farmers are in debt, and often must sell their land in order to cancel debt. During the last twenty years, South Korea moved from being a nearly food sufficient country to producing only 47 percent of its food needs. During the same period it became a major exporter of rice to the United States.

It is to these landless poor of the world that the church must respond. It is to them that it must fulfill with concrete action the promise of Jesus, "the poor shall inherit the land." On the fulfillment of that promise hinges the salvation of all.

Notes

1. LAND AND JUSTICE IN LATIN AMERICA

1. See Cheryl A. Lassen, *Landlessness and Rural Poverty in Latin America: Conditions, Trends and Policies Affecting Income and Employment* (Ithaca, N.Y.: Rural Development Committee, Center for International Studies, Cornell University, 1980). For an excellent overview of the problem of land and agrarian policy in Latin America, see Merilee S. Grindle, *State and Countryside, Development Policy and Agrarian Politics in Latin America* (Baltimore and London: Johns Hopkins University Press, 1986).

2. Roger Burbach and Patricia Flynn, *Agribusiness in the Americas* (New York: Monthly Review Press-North American Congress on Latin America, 1980), p. 14.

3. Gerritt Huizer, *The Revolutionary Potential of Peasants in Latin America* (Lexington, Mass.: Lexington Books, 1972), p. 1.

4. Tristan Platt, *Estado boliviano y ayllu andino, Tierra y tributo en el norte de Potosí* (Lima: Instituto de Estudios Peruanos, 1982), p. 15.

5. Ibid., p. 75.

6. Ernest Feder, *The Rape of the Peasantry, Latin America's Landholding System* (Garden City, N.Y.: Anchor Books, Doubleday, 1971), p. 109.

7. Ibid., p. 110.

8. Ibid., p. 88.

9. It is important to recognize that there are differences among rural peoples. "Peasants," discussed somewhat in detail in chapter 2, exhibit characteristics of a specific mode of production, focused around the family and village, with only marginal market participation. "Small farmers," who may or may not own land, are tied to the market economy, although seldom are able to accumulate capital. "Amerindian tribals" are indigenous groups who live outside capitalism and whose

way of life still largely is nomadic hunting and gathering, with only intermittent agriculture. Other differentiations should be made: salaried agricultural workers forming a true proletariat; part-time workers who might be termed "semiproletarian"; and squatters, renters, and sharecroppers, among others. For purposes of this essay, the phrase "peasants, small farmers, and Amerindians" attempts to summarize these differences; likewise the title, "the poor of the land" implies all marginal rural groups.

10. Burbach and Flynn, *Agribusiness in the Americas*, pp. 147, 149, 161.

11. Land tenure statistics on the Central American countryside have been gleaned from various sources analyzing the national situations, as well as newspaper articles and various reports. They are based mainly on agricultural censuses taken in 1974, 1979, and 1984, depending on the country. Since such censuses are taken perhaps only once every decade, and since they can be interpreted in various ways, the tabulations often vary slightly from report to report; they also tend to be "dated" because of their infrequency. At best, but in an important way, such statistics indicate trends and give an overview of the situation. The data on El Salvador comes from Robert G. Williams, *Export Agriculture and the Crisis in Central America* (Chapel Hill and London: University of North Carolina Press, 1986), p. 170. In addition to the Williams book, an excellent overview of the Central American situation and land is Charles D. Brockett, *Land, Power, and Poverty, Agrarian Transformation and Political Conflict in Central America* (Boston: Unwin Hyman, 1988).

12. Mitchell Allan Seligson, *Peasants of Costa Rica and the Development of Agrarian Capitalism* (Madison: University of Wisconsin Press, 1980), pp. 168-169.

13. *Tierra, estructura productiva y poder en Santa Cruz* (La Paz: Grupo de Estudios Andrés Ibañez, 1983), p. 22.

14. Recent analysis of Bolivia's land tenure systems are: *Tenencia de la Tierra rural en Bolivia—Problemas de la Reforma Agraria*, Boletín Documentación no. 17 (Julio 1987), CEPROLAI, La Paz, Bolivia; and Miguel Urioste F. de C., *Segunda Reforma Agraria: Campesinos, tierra y educación popular* (La Paz: CEDLA, 1987).

15. Lassen, *Landlessness*, p. 103. A good discussion of the small farmer in Brazil is Shepard Foreman, *The Brazilian Peasantry* (New York: Columbia University Press, 1975).

16. Comissão Pastoral da Terra, *CPT: Pastoral e Compromisso* (Petrópolis, Brazil: Editora Vozes, Comissão Pastoral da Terra, 1983). See chapter 1 for data on Brazil's landholding patterns.

17. Lassen, *Landlessness*, p. 103.

18. *Pela Vida no Nordeste* (Goiânia, Brazil: Comissão Pastoral da Terra, 1974), p. 34.

19. IBASE, "Concentração Fundiaria no Nordeste," Rio de Janeiro, 1982; folder containing statistics. See also IBASE, *Os Donos da Terra e a luta pela Reforma Agraria* (Rio de Janeiro: Editora Codecri, 1984), pp. 73–89.

20. Alexander Luzardo, "Ecocidio y Etnocidio en la Amazonia," *Nueva Sociedad* 53 (March/April 1981), p. 54.

21. For example, "45 percent of the Parakana died in the first months after the Transamazon cut through their territory. . . . Epidemic disease appears to be the major causative factor of this dispopulation" (Emilio F. Moran, *Developing the Amazon* [Bloomington: Indiana University Press, 1981], p. 42).

22. Shelton H. Davis, *Victims of the Miracle; Development and the Indians of Brazil* (Cambridge: Cambridge University Press, 1977), pp. 74–76.

23. Luzardo, "Ecocidio y Etnocidio," p. 54.

24. Davis, *Victims*, pp. 167–68. For general documentation, see the yearly reports compiled and published by the Centro Ecuménico de Documentação e Informação (CEDI), Rio de Janeiro, Brazil.

25. Foreman, *Brazilian Peasantry*, pp. 110–111.

26. Among the transnational corporations with interests, including mining, in this area and throughout the whole Amazon region, are Liquifarm (Italy); Volkswagon (West Germany); National Bulk Carriers (USA); Georgia Pacific (USA); Bethlehem Steel (USA); Alcoa (USA); Kaiser Aluminum (USA); Toyo Menka (Japan); Heublein Inc. (USA); King Ranch (USA); Sifco Industries, Inc. (USA); Dow Chemical (USA); Mitsui Co. (Japan); Twin Agricultural and Industrial Developers (USA); TRW Thompson (USA); Toshio Toyobo (Japan); Whirlpool Corporation (USA); Singer (USA); Union International (England); British Petroleum (England); Brascan (Canada); Anglo-American (South Africa); Utah-GE (USA); US Steel (USA); INCO (Canada); Royal Dutch Shell (Holland); Rio Tinto Zinc (England).

27. Such as ten-year tax exemptions, 50 percent tax reductions on corporate profits reinvested in Amazonia, and exemptions of farm machinery from import duties.

28. Two-thirds of the Nambiguara in Mato Grosso died in the 1970s due to the expansion of ranching. Moran, *Developing the Amazon*, p. 42. The Xavantes suffered a similar fate. Davis, *Victims*, p. 113.

29. *Paraguay, Power Game* (London: Latin American Bureau, 1980), pp. 47–56.

30. Ghislaine Duque, "A Experiência de Sobradinho: Problemas Fundiarios colocados pelas Grandes Barragems," *Cadernos do CEAS* 91 (May/June 1984), pp. 30–38.

31. Davis, *Victims*, pp. 79-82.

32. See IBASE, *Carajás, O Brasil Hipoteca seu Futuro* (Rio de Janeiro: Achiame, 1983).

33. Colonization, or new lands development, also destroys forests, although it is now realized that slash-and-burn agriculture is sound tropical agriculture if it remains within certain limits. Colonists do invade Amerindian lands, causing severe conflicts. Nevertheless, it must be remembered that the "need" for colonization is the refusal of genuine land reform that would signify land redistribution in the "colonist's" place of origin. Colonization is a symptom, not a cause of the problem.

34. Data supplied by the Oficina de Acción Social de la Iglesia, Santa Cruz, Bolivia, 1984.

35. The laborer's relationship always is with the contractor, never the actual owner.

36. Such practices have been reported regularly in the press throughout the 1980s. They also are well documented by various social action and advocacy agencies, including the CPT.

37. Feder, *Rape of the Peasantry,* pp. 171–254.

38. See Adelfo Martín Barrios, "Historia política de los campesinos cubanos"; Pablo González Casanova (coord.), *Historia de los Campesinos latinoamericanos*, I (Mexico City: Siglo Veintiuno, 1984), pp. 40–92; and Jean Le Coz, *Las Reformas Agrarias, de Zapata a Mao Tsé-tung y la FAO* (Barcelona: Editorial Ariel, 1976), pp. 171–76.

39. Pedro Negre Rigol and others, *Reformas Agrarias en América Latina (Mexico, Bolivia, Cuba, Chile, Peru)* (Buenos Aires: Tierra Nueva, 1976), p. 17.

40. Ibid., pp. 29–48. See also Javier Albó, *¿Bodas de Plata? O Requiem por una Reforma Agraria* (La Paz: CIPCA, 1979); Danilo Paz Ballivian, *Estructura agraria boliviana* (La Paz: Libreria Editorial "Popular," 1983); and the classic work, Dwight B. Heath, Charles J. Erasmus, and Hans C. Buechler, *Land Reform and Social Revolution in Bolivia* (New York: Frederick Praeger, 1969). The book by Urioste and the CEDCA *Boletín* give good contemporary analyses of the results of Bolivian land reform.

41. Pedro Casaldáliga and others, *Profetas, Tierra y Capitalismo, Iglesia y Campesinado en América Latina* (Bogotá: Centro de Investigación y Educación Popular, 1981), p. 175.

42. Francisco Barahona Riera, *Reforma Agraria y Poder Político* (San

José: Editorial Universidad de Costa Rica, 1980), p. 270. In fact, Costa Rica does not have agrarian reform. It does have a land program through which the government obtains land and resells it to land-needy peasants. However, the structure of property ownership remains untouched.

43. See Charles D. Brockett, *Land, Power, and Poverty: Agrarian Transformation and Political Conflict in Central America* (Boston: Unwin Hyman, 1988), pp. 154–62. For a study of peasant life, rural reality, and rebellion, see Jenny Pearce, *Promised Land: Peasant Rebellion in Chalatenango El Salvador* (London: Latin America Bureau, 1986); for land reform, see pp. 289–305.

44. See Brockett, *Land, Power, and Poverty*, pp. 169–86. My discussion closely follows his. See also Central American Historical Institute (Managua), *Envío* 37 (July 1984), and *Envío* 51 (September 1985); and Ilja A. Luciak, "Popular Hegemony and National Unity: The Dialectics of Sandinista Agrarian Reform Policies, 1979–1986," *LASA Forum* (Winter 1987), pp. 15–19.

45. Feder, *Rape of the Peasantry*, p. 19.

46. Williams, *Export Agriculture and the Crisis in Central America*, clearly demonstrates their correlation. It is a central theme of his excellent book.

47. Many international human rights organizations, including Amnesty International and Cultural Survival, have documented the terrible violence against Amerindian peasants. See Robert M. Carmack, ed., *Harvest of Violence: The Maya Indians and the Guatemalan Crisis* (Norman: University of Oklahoma Press, 1988). The relationship of massacres to land is one of the conclusions of the special report, "Las masacres como síntoma de descomposición social. Caso: El Aguacate, Chimaltenango" (Guatemala City: Centro de Investigación, Estudio, y Promoción de los Derechos Humanos, 1989). The report states that massacres are "a regular conduct that the majority of the times is employed to expel people from their land . . . used by landowners and the army . . . against the peasant population."

48. Feder, *Rape of the Peasantry*, p. 128.

49. See Elías Fajardo, *En Julgamento, a violência no campo* (Petrópolis: Instituto Apoio Jurídico Popular—Vozes—Fase, 1988). In Brazil, many studies of rural violence have been published, especially by church-related organizations. The CPT annually publishes reports on the year's violence. This violence has continued even in the democratic period of the New Republic. Over 800 murders have been committed since 1985.

50. The Comissão Pastoral da Terra lists nearly thirty government

agencies, see Comissão Pastoral da Terra, *CPT: Pastoral e Compromisso,* p. 29.

51. Ibid.

2. DEVELOPMENT THEORY AND LANDLESSNESS

1. Not all agro-industry has agriculture as its primary concern. For instance, petroleum/chemical companies produce and sell agrichemicals. They also are involved in other aspects of agricultural production as a lucrative sideline, among others, seeds. Royal Dutch Shell, Union Carbide, Celanese, Ciba-Geigy, even the communications company ITT, among others, are the owners of major seed companies. These nonseed seed companies maintain almost monopolistic control over the sale and development, including genetic research, of seed varieties, determining what is available and not available. Varieties also are developed that respond only to the company's chemical products, thus assuring even more control. See Pat Roy Mooney, *Seeds of the Earth, A Private or Public Resource?* (Ottawa: Inter Pares for the Canadian Council for International Co-operation and the International Coalition for Development Action in London), 1979; idem, "The Law of the Seed, Modern Development and Plant Genetic Resources," *Development Dialogue* 1–2 (1983); and Cary Fowler, Eva Lachkovics, Pat Mooney, and Hope Shand, "The Laws of Life, Modern Development and the New Biotechnologies," *Development Dialogue* 1–2 (1988).

2. Jeffrey Ashe, *Rural Development in Costa Rica* (New York: Interbook, Acción Internacional, 1978), p. 47.

3. IBASE, "Agricultura no Brasil: Produção para Consumo Interno y Produção para Exportação" (mimeographed paper).

4. "Tenencia de la tierra rural en Bolivia, Problema de la Reforma Agraria," *Boletín Documentación* no. 17 (July 1987), CEPROLAI, La Paz, Bolivia, p. 20.

5. A.T. Mosher, *To Create a Modern Agriculture, Organization and Planning* (New York: Agricultural Development Council, 1971), p. 79.

6. Hollis Chenery and others, *Redistribution with Growth* (New York: Oxford University Press for the World Bank/Institute of Development Studies, University of Sussex, 1974), esp. chapter 2.

7. The pioneering study also emphasizing the importance of human resources is T.W. Schultz, *Transforming Traditional Agriculture* (New Haven: Yale University Press, 1964).

8. Gunnar Myrdal, *Challenge of World Poverty: A World Antipoverty Program in Outline* (New York: Pantheon Books, Random House, 1970), p. 88.

9. Ibid., p. 86.

10. *Boletín* de CEPROLAI, p. 20.

11. Ernest Feder, *The Rape of the Peasantry,* pp. 101f.; James P. Grant, "Growth from Below: A People-oriented Development Strategy," *Development Paper* 16 (Washington, D.C.: Overseas Development Council). This has been my personal experience working with Andean peasants.

12. The original theoretical model was conceived by A.V. Chayanov, edited by D. Thorner, R.E.F. Smith, and B. Kerbloy, *The Theory of Peasant Economy* (Homewood, Ill.: Richard D. Irwin, Inc., 1966), who developed the theory while serving as director of the Institute of Agricultural Economy in the Soviet Union following the 1917 revolution. See also the important book by Teodor Shanin, ed., *Peasants and Peasant Societies: Selected Readings* (Middlesex, England: Penguin Books, 1971). My own empirical reference upon which this discussion is developed is the Aymara-Quechua peasants of the Bolivian highlands.

13. See Henry Bernstein, "Concepts for the Analysis of Contemporary Peasantries," in Rosemary G. Galli, ed., *The Political Economy of Rural Development: Peasants, International Capital and the State* (Albany: State University of New York Press, 1981).

14. Davydd J. Greenwood, *The Political Economy of Peasant Family Farming: Some Anthropological Perspectives on Rationality and Adaptation* (Ithaca, N.Y.: Rural Development Committee, Center for International Studies, Cornell University, 1973), p. 30.

15. Eric R. Wolf, *Peasants* (Englewood Cliffs, N.J.: Prentice Hall, 1966). This historicist position is developed by Shanin; it is the argument Greenwood makes.

16. Bernstein, "Concepts," p. 18.

17. Greenwood, *The Political Economy of Peasant Family Farming,* pp. 30, 61.

18. Ibid., p. 69.

19. For a discussion of land reform theory in Latin America, see Antonio García, *Modelos Operacionales de reforma agraria y desarrollo rural en América Latina* (San José: Instituto Interamericano de Cooperación para la Agricultura [IICA], 1985).

20. What few economists or social scientists recognize is that their work is always laden with underlying value assumptions. They are never purely "scientific" or "technical."

3. LAND IN THE BIBLICAL TRADITION

1. This and the other popular readings of biblical texts found in this chapter are from "El campesino lee la Biblia," *El Pueblo hace el*

camino: Una lectura Latinoamericana de la Biblia, no. 2 (1988), publication of the program on Bible of the Latin American Network of the CCPD, WCC, São Paulo, Brazil. The English translations are mine.

2. Marcelo de Barros, José Luis Caravias, *Teología de la tierra* (São Paulo: Ediciones Paulinas, 1988), pp. 128, 8.

3. Walter Brueggemann, *The Land* (Philadelphia: Fortress, 1977), p. 3.

4. Marcelo de Barros Souza, *A Biblia e a Luta Pela Terra*(Petrópolis: Vozes-Comisão pastoral da Terra, 1983). Also see: Javier Pikaza, *La Biblia y la Teología de la Historia* (Madrid: Ediciones FAX, 1972).

5. W.D. Davies, *The Gospel and the Land: Early Christianity and Jewish Territorial Doctrine* (Berkeley: University of California Press, 1974); Antonio Gonzáles Lamadrid, *La fuerza de la tierra, Geografía, historia y teología de palestina* (Salamanca: Ediciones Sígueme, 1981); Norman K. Gottwald, *The Tribes of Yahweh* (Maryknoll, N.Y.: Orbis Books, 1979).

6. Gerhard von Rad, *The Problem of the Hexateuch and Other Essays* (New York: McGraw-Hill, 1966), p. 79.

7. Ernst Jenni and Claus Westermann, *Diccionario Teológico del Antiguo Testamento* (Madrid: Ediciones Cristiandad, 1978), pp. 110–15.

8. Brueggemann, *The Land*, p. 2.

9. Patrick D. Miller, Jr., "The Gift of God," *Interpretation* vol. 23, no. 4 (October 1969), p. 454.

10. Von Rad, *The Problem of the Hexateuch*, p. 93.

11. Miller, "The Gift of God," p. 543.

12. Ibid., p. 455.

13. Ibid., p. 456.

14. Gottwald, *The Tribes of Yahweh*, pp. 191–233, 489–492.

15. This is Gottwald's conclusion, first suggested by George E. Mendenhall, *The Tenth Generation: The Origins of the Biblical Tradition* (Baltimore: Johns Hopkins University Press, 1973). George V. Pixley, *God's Kingdom: A Guide for Biblical Study* (Maryknoll, N.Y.: Orbis Books, 1981), concurs.

16. Jorge V. Pixley, *Historia sagrada, Historia popular: Historia de Israel desde los pobres (1220 a.C. a 135d.C.)* (San José: DEI-CIEETS, 1989), pp. 12, 14.

17. Gottwald and Pixley describe in some detail this system.

18. Gottwald, *The Tribes of Yahweh*, pp. 480-482.

19. Ibid., p. 212.

20. Ibid.

21. Apparently the *apiru* were rebellious, guerrilla outlaws for hire,

in the service of one ruling dynasty or city-state against another, but also always ready to turn on their employer. As an expression of deep social discontent in Canaan, the *apiru* were a disruptive force in the Canaanite tributary system and Egyptian imperialism. See Gottwald, *The Tribes of Yahweh,* pp. 397, 401–9, for an extended discussion.

22. Eric R. Wolf, "On Peasant Rebellions," in Teodor Shanin, ed., *Peasants and Peasant Societies: Selected Readings* (Middlesex, England, and New York: Penguin Books, 1971, 1973, 1976), p. 273.

23. From the scripture it is evident that slaves and day laborers augmented the work force of the wealthy. Nevertheless, use of external labor was the exception, not the norm. The sabbatical-jubilee provision for freeing of slaves, debt peons, etc., shows that external nonfamily labor finally was unacceptable. Gottwald defines *mishpehah* as "protective association of families" who provided various kinds of mutual services (see pp. 257–84). Such mutual assistance structured into the social order is characteristic of peasant societies. A contemporary expression is the *ayni* of the Andean peoples.

24. Pixley, *Historia sagrada, Historia popular,* p. 20.

25. Wolf, "On Peasant Rebellions," p. 272.

26. Von Rad, *The Problem of the Hexateuch,* pp. 85–88.

27. Jenni, Westermann, *Diccionario Teológico,* pp. 1068–73.

28. Von Rad, *The Problem of the Hexateuch,* p. 85.

29. Ibid., p. 263.

30. Ibid., p. 253.

31. Gerhard von Rad, *Genesis, A Commentary* (Philadelphia: Westminster, 1961), pp. 74–75.

32. Gunter A. Wolff, "A Historia da Luta entre o Pastor Abel e o Agricultor Caim," *Tempo e presença* no. 182 (May 1983), pp. 22–24.

33. Walter Brueggemann, *Genesis* (Atlanta: John Knox, 1982), pp. 130–32. See also Von Rad, *Genesis,* pp. 165–69.

34. Gottwald, *The Tribes of Yahweh,* p. 389.

35. Ibid.

36. Johannes Bauer, *Diccionario de la Teología Bíblica* (Barcelona: Editorial Herder, 1966), pp. 225–56.

37. Brueggemann, *Genesis,* pp. 35–36.

38. It is unknown to what degree the sabbath and jubilee years actually were practiced. Generally scholars have assumed that they remained mostly theoretical measures for achieving social justice, especially the jubilee. More recent investigation, however, suggests that they were practiced historical events. See Jacob Milgrom, "The Book of Leviticus," in Charles M. Laymon, ed., *The Interpreter's One-Volume Commentary on the Bible* (Nashville: Abingdon, 1971), pp. 82–83.

39. Milgrom, "Leviticus," p. 83; John Howard Yoder, *The Politics of Jesus* (Grand Rapids: William B. Eerdmans, 1978), p. 222.

40. Von Rad, *Problem of the Hexateuch*, pp. 85ff.

41. Andrés Kirk, "Cada uno bajo su vid y bajo su higuera, la búsqueda de una hermenéutica pertinente," *Revista Bíblica* no. 173 (1979), p. 165.

42. G. Johannes Botterweck and Homer Ringgren, eds., *Theological Dictionary of the Old Testament* (Grand Rapids: Eerdmans, 1978), p. 222.

43. See Jon Douglas Levenson, *Theology of the Program of Restoration of Ezekiel 40–48* (Missoula, Mont.: Scholar's Press, 1976), especially pp. 111–25.

44. Pikaza, *La Biblia y la teología de la Historia*, p. 317.

45. Ibid.

46. Antonio Gonzáles Lamadrid, *La fuerza de la tierra, geografía, historia y teología de Palestina* (Salamanca: Ediciones Sígueme, 1981), p. 186.

47. Davies, *The Gospel and the Land*, p. 367.

48. Victor Paul Furnish, "The Letter of Paul to the Ephesians," in Laymon, *The Interpreter's One-Volume Commentary on the Bible*, p. 837.

49. Brueggemann, *The Land*, p. 178.

50. Ibid.

51. Warren A. Quanbeck, "The Letter to the Hebrews," in Laymon, *The Interpreter's One-Volume Commentary on the Bible*, p. 903.

52. Roy I. Sano, *Outside the Gate: A Study of the Letter to the Hebrews* (New York: General Board of Global Ministries, Education and Cultivation Division for the Women's Division, 1982), pp. 42, 48.

53. Sophie Laws, *A Commentary on the Epistle of James* (San Francisco: Harper & Row, 1980), p. 201.

54. Joachim Jeremias, *Jerusalem in the Time of Jesus: An Investigation into Economic and Social Conditions during the New Testament Period* (Philadelphia: Fortress, 1969), p. 111.

55. Laws, *Commentary on the Epistle of James*, p. 202.

56. Brueggemann, *The Land*, p. 170.

57. Thomas D. Hanks, *God So Loved the Third World: The Biblical Vocabulary of Oppression* (Maryknoll, N. Y.: Orbis Books, 1983), chapter 4; Yoder, *The Politics of Jesus,* chapter 3. See also the fertile article by Mortimer Arias, "Mission and Liberation, The Jubilee: A Paradigm for Mission Today," *International Review of Mission* vol. 73, no. 289 (January 1984). For an excellent theological ethical discussion of the connection between Jubilee and Jesus' reign preaching, see Sharon H. Ringe, *Jesus, Liberation and the Biblical Jubilee, Images for Ethics and Christology* (Philadelphia: Fortress, 1985).

58. Joachim Jeremias, *The Parables of Jesus* (London: SCM Press, 1961), pp. 58–59.

59. Jeremias, *Jerusalem in the Time of Jesus,* chapters 1, 2.

60. Richard A. Horsley and John S. Hanson, *Bandits, Prophets and Messiahs. Popular Movements in the Time of Jesus* (Minneapolis: Winston, 1985).

61. Alberto Ricciardi, "Los Pobres y la Tierra según el Salmo 37," *Revista Bíblica* no. 174 (1979/4).

62. Johannes B. Bauer, *Diccionario de Teología Bíblica* (Barcelona: Editorial Herder, 1967), p. 830; Xavier Leon-Dufour, *Dictionary of Biblical Theology,* second edition (New York: Seabury, 1973), pp. 436–37.

63. J. Severino Croatto, "Los Oprimidos Poseerán la Tierra (Recontextualización de un tema bíblico)," *Revista Bíblica* no. 174 (1979/4). Also Ricciardi, "Los Pobres y la Tierra."

64. Yoder, *The Politics of Jesus,* p. 68.

65. Ibid.

66. Gustavo Gutiérrez, *We Drink from Our Own Wells: The Spiritual Journey of a People* (Maryknoll, N. Y.: Orbis Books, 1984), pp. 77–78.

67. Wolf, "On Peasant Rebellions," p. 273.

4. THE CHURCH AND THE CHALLENGE OF LAND

1. François Chevalier, *Land and Society in Colonial Mexico: The Great Hacienda* (Berkeley and Los Angeles: University of California Press, 1963), p. 234.

2. Norman H. Dabbs, *Dawn over the Bolivian Hills* (Canadian Baptist Foreign Mission Board, 1952), pp. 183–84.

3. Central Committee, "Land Rights for Indigenous People," in *Land Rights for Indigenous People,* PCR Information, reports and background papers, no. 16 (World Council of Churches—Program to Combat Racism, March 1983), pp. 10–11.

4. Consejo Latinoamericano de Iglesias, *Porque de ellos es la Tierra: El derecho a la tierra de los pueblos aborígenes* (Mexico: Casa Unida de Publicaciones, 1983), p. 8.

5. *Latinamerica Press,* March 10, 1988.

6. "El clamor de los obispos," *Crónica,* April 7, 1988, p. 14.

7. Richard Aitkenhead Castillo, "Tierra, pobreza y oportunidades," ibid., p. 16.

8. Pablo R. Schneider, Hugo Maul, and Luis Mauricio Membreño, *El mito de la Reforma Agraria, 40 años de experimentación en Guatemala* (Guatemala City: Centro de Investigaciones Económicas Nacionales, March 1989), p. 52. See also Lionel Toriello Nájera, *El clamor por una*

vida mejor: Análisis de la estrategia de Desarrollo que debe adoptar Guatemala a la luz de un enfoque sobre su realidad agraria (Guatemala City: Asociación de Amigos del País, February 1989).

9. "El clamor de los obispos," *Crónica*, April 7, 1988, p. 12.

5. THE BRAZILIAN CHURCH AND STRUGGLE FOR LAND

1. For a historical summary of church documents, see *Brasil: ¿Para quién es la tierra? Solidaridad de la iglesia con los "sin tierra"* (Lima: Centro de Estudios y Publicaciones, 1984).

2. Actually there is not a contradiction, because the bishops base their analysis on the concept of peasant economy as is explained in chapter 2.

3. Pedro Casaldáliga, "Comentarios al Documento 'Iglesia y Problemas de la Tierra en Brasil,'" *Profetas, Tierra y Capitalismo: Iglesia y Campesinado en America Latina* (Bogotá: Centro de Investigación y Educación Popular, 1981), p. 110.

4. *Visión*, November 15/29, 1982, p. 29.

5. Comissão Pastoral da Terra, *CPT: Pastoral e Compromiso* (Petrópolis: Editora Vozes—Comissão Pastoral da Terra, 1983), p. 88.

6. Ibid., p. 7.

7. Ibid., p. 78.

8. Ibid., p. 80.

9. Final Document, IV National Assembly of CIMI, *Boletim do CIMI* (July-August 1981), p. 11.

10. Pablo Suess, *Culturas Indígenas y evangelización* (Lima: Centro de Estudios y Publicaciones, 1983), pp. 55–56.

11. Ibid., p. 75

12. Edgar Jorge Kolling, "Romeria da Terra," *Tempo e presença*, July 1987, p. 21.

13. Ibid., p. 22

14. See Carlos Enrique Guanziroli and Isabella Fernandes, *Reforma agrária em terras da igreja, São Miguel: relato de uma experiencia* (Petrópolis: Editora Vozes, 1987).

15. *Latinamerica Press*, October 24, 1985.

16. *Pe. Josimo: a velha violência da Nova Republica* (Comissão Pastoral da Terra, 1986), p. 18.

17. Dom Erwin Krautler, "Os povos indígenas e a igreja missionária neste crucial momento historico," *Cadernos do CEAS*, no. 117 (September-October 1988), pp. 52–53.

18. *Aconteceu no mundo evangélico*, no. 46, May 1986.

19. The stories of Father Jentel and those that follow in this section

have been recounted in various publications. See particularly Penny Lernoux, *Cry of the People: United States Involvement in the Rise of Fascism, Torture and Murder and Persecution of the Catholic Church in Latin America* (Garden City, N.Y.: Doubleday, 1980). Brazilian publications include: Ricardo Rezende Figueira, *A justiça do Lobo, Posseiros e padres do Araguaia* (Petrópolis: Editora Vozes, 1986); and Neide Esterci, *Conflito no Araguaia, Peoes e posseiros contra a grande empresa* (Petrópolis: Editora Vozes, 1987). In 1984 I visited the region as part of the research for this book.

20. Pe. Josimo, *a velha violência da Nova Republica*, p. 93.

21. *Aconteceu no mundo evangélico*, no. 70, September 1988.

6. LAND AND MINISTRY

1. Walter Brueggemann, *The Land* (Philadelphia: Fortress, 1977), p. 3, says that land is a "prism" for understanding biblical faith.

2. David L. Ostendorf, "Who will control rural America? Food, land, people and power," *Christianity and Crisis* (May 2, 1988), p. 159.

3. This is a fundamental principle for Nicaraguan agrarian reform following the Sandinista revolution.

4. For an overall discussion of collective farming models, see Peter Dorner, ed., *Cooperative and Commune: Group Farming in the Economic Development of Agriculture* (Madison: University of Wisconsin Press, 1977).

5. Claus Westermann, *Creation* (Philadelphia: Fortress, 1974), pp. 50–55.

6. Thomas Sieger Derr, *Ecology and Human Liberation: A Theological Critique of the Use and Abuse of Our Birthright* (Geneva: World Council of Churches—World Student Christian Federation, 1977), p. 66.

7. Ibid., pp. 47–48.

8. Ibid., p. 69.

9. C. Dean Freudenberger, *Food for Tomorrow?* (Minneapolis: Augsburg, 1984), pp. 97–106. This trilateral framework comes from the World Council of Churches, which developed this theme in both theological and technical terms during the early 1980s.

10. Ostendorf, *Christianity and Crisis*, p. 157.

11. Brueggemann, *The Land*, p. 35.

12. Ibid., p. 38.

13. Ibid., p. 100.

EPILOGUE

1. Ron Moreau and Sudip Mazumbar, "A Grim Journey to the 'Other India,' " *Newsweek*, June 15, 1987.

Of Related Interest

Paul Vallely
BAD SAMARITANS
First World Ethics and Third World Debt

A British journalist, determined to understand the tragedy of the Ethiopian famine, began an in-depth investigation of the international economy. The legacies of colonialism and development strategies that breed more dependency; the effects of the budget deficits in the U.S. and rising interest rates; the draconian policies of the IMF and the World Bank: Vallely paints a devastating picture of the human cost of all these economic factors. From there, he turns to the Bible and Christian tradition to find the resources for a different view of economics "as if people mattered."

"A really readable book." —**Bob Geldof**

200pp. ISBN 0-88344-685-5 Paperback

Jack Nelson-Pallmeyer
WAR AGAINST THE POOR
Low Intensity Conflict and Christian Faith
Includes a Postscript on the 1990 Nicaraguan Elections

Shows how the poor of Central America are victimized by a "unified package" of economic, diplomatic, and military interference designed to block social change. LIC not only disables the poor, but threatens to undermine U.S. democracy—and Christian faith.

"The war in Central America isn't just a shooting war. . . . Jack's book is the best tool we have for getting that message across."
                        —**Ed Griffen-Nolan, Witness for Peace**

130pp. ISBN 0-88344-589-1 Paperback

Thomas P. Fenton and Mary J. Heffron
FOOD, HUNGER, AGRIBUSINESS
A Directory of Resources

Hundreds of annotated entries describe organizations, print, and AV materials for teaching and learning not only about the perennial "hunger" of the Third World, but efforts to grow and distribute more food and the role international corporations play in every aspect of food production, distribution, and consumption.

"Deserves, and I hope it receives, a wide audience."
—Arthur Simon, Bread for the World

150pp. ISBN 0-88344-660-X Paperback

Sean McDonagh
THE GREENING OF THE CHURCH

For the author of *To Care for the Earth* third world debt and the despoiling of the natural environment are entwined in a skein of remarkable toughness that resists faint-hearted attempts to unravel it. McDonagh argues that ecology must be put at the center of Christian theology, and suggests a Christian approach to the ecosystem that envisages human nature as part of the divine cosmic whole. He then shows how we must accept the humility of creaturehood, while also exercising stewardship within creation.

"A very important work. . . ."**—John F. Haught**

300pp. ISBN 0-88344-694-4 Paperback